Myths and Realities about the Decentralization of Health Systems

Other Books by Management Sciences for Health

Beyond the Clinic Walls: Case Studies in Community-Based Distribution, ed. James A. Wolff et al. (W. Hartford, CT: Kumarian Press)

CORE—Cost and Revenue Analysis Tool

Family Planning Management Terms: A Pocket Glossary in Three Languages, by Janice Miller and Claire Bahamon

The Family Planning Manager's Handbook: Basic Skills and Tools for Managing Family Planning Programs, ed. James A. Wolff, Linda J. Suttenfield, and Susanna C. Binzen (W. Hartford, CT: Kumarian Press)

Health Care in Muslim Asia: Development and Disorder in Wartime Afghanistan, ed. Ronald W. O'Connor

Health Financing Reform in Kenya: The Fall and Rise of Cost Sharing, 1989–94, ed. David Collins et al.

Lessons from FPMD: Decentralizing the Management of Health and Family Planning Programs, by Riitta-Liisa Kolehmainen-Aitken and William Newbrander

Lessons from FPMD: Developing Information Systems for Managing Family Planning Programs, by Riitta-Liisa Kolehmainen-Aitken et al.

Management Strategies for Improving Family Planning Services: The Family Planning Manager Compendium, ed. Janice Miller and James A. Wolff

Managing Drug Supply: The Selection, Procurement, Distribution, and Use of Pharmaceuticals, with the World Health Organization, second edition, revised and expanded (W. Hartford, CT: Kumarian Press)

Private Health Sector Growth in Asia: Issues and Implications, ed. William Newbrander (Chichester, England: John Wiley & Sons)

Myths and Realities about the Decentralization of Health Systems

edited by Riitta-Liisa Kolehmainen-Aitken

MSH **MANAGEMENT SCIENCES FOR HEALTH**
Boston

Copyright © 1999 Management Sciences for Health, Inc.
All rights reserved.

Management Sciences for Health
165 Allandale Rd.
Boston, MA 02130-3400

Tel: 617/524-7799
Fax: 617/524-2825
Web site: www.msh.org
Orders: fpmdpubs@msh.org

0-913723-56-8 hardcover
0-913723-52-5 paper

Original version of chapter 3, "Decentralization and Human Resources: Implications and Impact," published in *Human Resources for Health Development Journal* 2(1): 1–16, 1998. Reprinted by permission.

The development of this publication was partially funded by the US Agency for International Development through the Family Planning Management Development project under cooperative agreement CCP-A-00-95-00000-02. The views expressed herein are those of the authors and do not necessarily reflect those of USAID.

Project editor: Barbara Timmons, MSH
Production manager: Jenna Dixon
Copyeditor: Linda Lotz
Typesetter: Sam Sheng
Proofreader: Beth Richards
Indexer: Jan Williams

Printed in the United States of America on acid-free paper by Malloy Lithographing Inc. with vegetable-oil based ink.

∞ The paper used in this publication meets the minimum requirements of the American National Standard for Information Sciences — Permanence of Paper for Printed Library Materials, ANSI Z39.48-1984.

Library of Congress Cataloging-in-Publication Data
Myths and realities about the decentralization of health systems / edited by
   Riitta-Liisa Kolehmainen-Aitken.
     p.   cm.
   Includes bibliographical references and index.
   ISBN 0-913723-56-8 (hardcover : alk. paper). — ISBN 0-913723-52-5
(pbk. : alk. paper)
    1. Public health administration—Decentralization—Developing countries.
2. Decentralization in government—Developing countries. 3. Health services administration—Developing countries.
I. Kolehmainen-Aitken, Riitta-Liisa.
RA395.D44.M97   1999
362.1'09172'4   99-25251

---

10 9 8 7 6 5 4 3 2 1   05 04 03 02 01 00 99

To conduct great matters and never commit a fault is above the force of human nature.
—*Plutarch*, Life of Fabius

Contents

Introduction 1

Part I   Technical Support   9

1   Planning for and within Decentralized Health Systems   11
    Malcolm Bryant

2   Financing, Service Delivery, and Decentralization in the Philippines and Kenya   27
    Charles C. Stover

3   Human Resources Development under Decentralization   39
    Riitta-Liisa Kolehmainen-Aitken

4   Pharmaceutical Management at the Central and Local Levels   65
    Richard Laing

5   A New Management Information Strategy for Decentralized Public Health Services in the Philippines   73
    Robert J. Timmons, Jose R. Rodriguez, and Florante P. Magboo

6   Does Decentralization Lead to Better-Quality Services?   95
    Steven Solter

Part II   Health Services   109

7   Implementation and Integration of Reproductive Health Services in a Decentralized System   111
    Iain W. Aitken

8   The Impact of Decentralization on Hospitals   137
    William Newbrander

Part III Case Study 155

9 Decentralization in Indonesia: An Evolutionary Process 157
   Robert S. Northrup

About the Contributors 170
Index 175
About Management Sciences for Health 183

Introduction

Riitta-Liisa Kolehmainen-Aitken

THE 1990S HAS WITNESSED a rapid rise in the number of countries that are decentralizing the management of their public-sector health delivery systems. Yet the term "decentralization" remains vague, denoting a wide variety of power-sharing relationships. Although public claims about the anticipated improvements in equity, quality, access, and efficiency are frequently made, the real implications of decentralization for health system performance remain poorly understood. The data to support these claims about promised benefits are still sparse. It is becoming clear, however, that politicians and advocates of decentralization frequently underestimate the complexity of designing and implementing the fundamental changes in management systems that decentralization, in whatever form, demands if health service delivery is to improve.

Equitable and efficient provision of health services that are readily available, appropriate, and of acceptable quality requires systematic health planning. It also depends on the smooth functioning of crucial technical support systems, such as those required for managing financial and human resources, pharmaceutical supplies, logistics, and essential management information. Decentralization inevitably affects how these systems are structured at the different management levels and thus has the potential to profoundly influence the capacity of these systems to support service provision.

Regrettably, decentralization's impact on these technical support areas is largely unexplored, and no consensus has yet emerged on how the different roles and responsibilities within these areas should optimally be divided among different management levels or entities.

The introduction of new policy directions is another sphere where decentralization's impact can be substantial. Examples of such new policy directions are the expanded reproductive health agenda that emerged from the 1994 International Conference on Population and Development in Cairo and the recent push for integrated management of childhood illness by WHO. Little international exchange of information or debate has taken place to explore the successes and challenges of such policy changes within a decentralized health care system.

This anthology is intended as a contribution to the international discussion on decentralization's impact on technical support areas, as well as on the introduction of new policy agendas. It arose from presentations at the 1997 American Public Health Association meeting in Indianapolis, Indiana, by staff members of Management Sciences for Health and their colleagues at the Harvard School of Public Health and Boston University. The writers are all experts with extensive real-world experience in their technical areas who have witnessed the changes that decentralization has brought to health care delivery in developing countries. In contributing to this anthology, their goal was not to write an academic treatise on decentralization but to share with others the practical lessons they have learned and the observations they have made when responding to the challenges of decentralization in their own particular fields of expertise.

The anthology is divided into three parts. The first part focuses on decentralization's impact on those technical support areas that are most important for the delivery of any type of health service. These include health planning, financing, human resources, pharmaceuticals, management information, and the improvement of service quality. The second part examines the relationship of decentralization to two key health service areas, namely, reproductive health and hospital services. The chapters in Parts I and II cite examples from many regions and specific countries. The third part is an in-depth review of the historical evolution of decentralization in Indonesia.

In the first chapter, Malcolm Bryant points out that decentralization is commonly politically driven. This can lead to many avoidable mistakes if planners are not given an opportunity to provide necessary input or if they lack sufficient information to understand the decentralization process. Planning *for* decentralization should be based on a clear understanding of the motivating and opposing forces for decentralization, as well as its explicit and implicit objectives. A functional definition of what decentralization means in the local context must be developed, and the legal framework adapted to suit. Planners must be prepared for new demands on management systems and skills and for the potentially increased capital and recurrent costs. The health planning roles and responsibilities of central and peripheral levels *under* decentralization are also discussed, and the chapter concludes with practical advice that can help a health planner introduce decentralization. Bryant emphasizes that managers must take the lead in shaping the new health system and gather good information on which to base their decisions. They must look for assistance and allies, be clear about their own role, and communicate it to others. Finally, they must ensure that their priorities are right and that their colleagues have been prepared for the challenges that decentralization brings.

Charles Stover compares the experience of financial management in the Philippines and in Kenya to demonstrate how different financial strategies can either lead decentralization or follow it. In the Philippines, the devolution of powers to the local government unit (LGU) level dramatically changed the public financing of health services. The formula used to divide the national revenue among LGUs failed to take into account the existing distribution of health facilities and programs, which resulted in a considerable financing gap in the provinces. The response to this rapidly emerging financial crisis was the development of innovative voluntary health insurance schemes in several provinces. The casualty was the breakdown of the national drug procurement system, since many provinces experienced severe delays in receiving drugs when drug procurement for public hospitals was incorporated into the regular provincial system for procuring other goods. Kenya, in contrast, had no political mandate for decentralization. A cost-sharing program was established in the

Ministry of Health, but with no specific policy intention of leading to decentralization. Through a slow and deliberate process of capacity building, many district and provincial boards are now beginning to improve services, using the financial systems that were established under the cost-sharing program. Although the overall political debate about the merits of decentralization continues in Kenya, a potential for increased decentralization has been established.

In the third chapter (originally published in *Human Resources for Health Development Journal*), Riitta-Liisa Kolehmainen-Aitken points out that decentralization can affect the human resources domain in two ways. Important human resources issues emerge as part of the process of transferring power to lower management levels. Foremost among such issues are the adequacy of available information on human resources, the complexity of staff transfer, the impact of unions and professional bodies, and the morale and motivation of staff. For example, personality conflict, mistrust, professional pride, and jealousy can all impede successful decentralization. Human resources problems also arise as a result of the way in which decentralized management systems are structured. Affected areas include the appropriateness of organizational structures, roles and responsibilities, viability of coordinated health and human resources development, sustainability of training capacity, maintenance of technical and managerial competence, and security of adequate performance conditions. Negative examples are presented to highlight the importance of considering human resources implications at every step of the decentralization process. Five practical recommendations are provided for health managers in decentralizing settings: (1) all managers should become human resources advocates; (2) they should anticipate the cost and complexity of the decentralization process as it relates to the human resources area; (3) a strategic human resources capability should be developed, with appropriate roles defined for both central and local levels; (4) a heavy investment in staff development is required for successful decentralization; (5) the impact of decentralization on human resources should be regularly monitored.

Richard Laing's chapter identifies the roles that national and local levels should play in six key areas of pharmaceutical policy and programming: selection, distribution, procurement, rational use, financing, and quality assurance. Advice on how the central government can help a process of decentralization is provided. The center should focus on defining a list of essential drugs and standard treatment guidelines, as well as establishing appropriate regulations and quality-assurance systems. It also has an important role in assisting local authorities, for example, by developing simple stock-management and financial systems, simple measures for drug testing, and more effective local procurement of essential drugs. Laing observes that decentralization may affect pharmaceutical supply profoundly and stresses that some aspects of pharmaceutical management, such as drug registration, should never be decentralized.

Robert Timmons, Jose Rodriguez, and Florante Magboo provide a detailed analysis of a new national strategy for monitoring and evaluating family planning and maternal and child health services in the Philippines. Prior to the devolution of power to the local government level, the national Department of Health used the Field Health Services Information System (FHSIS) to collect and consolidate client information from 17 primary health care programs. The emphasis of the FHSIS on data consolidation for the national level and its dependence on computerization made it ill suited for the postdevolution era. In its new role, the Department of Health requires data on the national situation as measured by program effects and impact. Local governments, which are now in charge of primary health service delivery, need information about the effects of these services on their communities, the level of utilization of these services, and the quality of care delivered. The new monitoring strategy, designed to respond to these needs, exploits a variety of data sources at different levels of the health care system. These include health facility assessments to monitor quality of care, health service statistics for local decision making, cluster surveys by LGUs and regional research institutions to measure program performance, and riders to the National Statistics Office's Labor Force Survey to assess population impact. In their conclusion, the authors raise the issue of sustainability of the management information strategy.

Steven Solter's chapter explores the theoretical connection between quality and decentralization. He points out that quality of services can be understood from three different perspectives: that of a manager, a health care provider, and a client. Several health system factors determine quality and can be affected by decentralization, including training of staff, their experience and motivation, drugs, equipment, health facility infrastructure, supervision and referral networks, and information and communication. In the Philippines, indirect evidence indicates that poor staff motivation and disruption of service delivery caused by the devolution of power had a substantial negative impact on health system performance. Immunization coverage of infants dropped from approximately 85 percent in 1993 to less than 80 percent in 1994. Vitamin A distribution to children one to five years of age fell off. Because previous travel allowances were abolished by most LGUs, the level of supervision declined. District hospitals, which now came under the provinces' jurisdiction, ceased supporting and supervising municipal health services. Solter observes that even when faced with these challenges, the national Department of Health continued to behave as if it were still responsible for providing direct primary health care services, instead of transforming itself into an organization responsible for managing service delivery. Four key lessons emerge from the Philippine experience. First, decentralization must be planned and its implications thoroughly understood prior to implementation if quality is not to be affected. Second, a change in roles and styles is just as important at the central level as at the local level. Third, frontline health workers must feel confident about the security of their jobs and benefits if they are to provide quality services. Fourth, a simple change in management practices, such as stopping the payment of a small travel allowance, can have an enormous and devastating impact on quality.

Iain Aitken's chapter shifts the focus from decentralization's impact on technical support areas to the challenges it brings to health programs and delivery structures. Its purpose is twofold. First, it considers both the process and the goals of the changes required to implement a new policy push—namely, expanded reproductive health services—within a decentralized health system. This includes review of increased opposition at local levels to government reproductive health policies. Second, it assesses the extent to which these goals are compatible or in conflict with those of decentralization. Both sets of policies (i.e., reproductive health and decentralization) involve notions of human rights and democratization and thus appear to be compatible. Aitken argues that the implementation of these policies requires three complementary approaches if the goals of expanded access to and enhanced quality of reproductive health services—which most countries aspire to—are to be achieved: (1) improving the client-provider interface, (2) developing functioning health systems, and (3) integrating reproductive health services, including the reintegration of family planning into the health sector. Their successful implementation depends on control over resources and government functions, the freedom and ability to respond to local situations, and the motives and methods of administrative and program integration. Decentralization can profoundly affect each of these areas. Aitken identifies several potential advantages of decentralization that can help achieve the Cairo Programme of Action. These include greater flexibility in integrating the different components of reproductive health to suit local needs, vertical integration between primary health care providers and hospitals, and improved community participation. He also cites several examples suggesting that in many countries the opposite has been true, and decentralization has not facilitated realization of the Cairo reproductive health agenda.

William Newbrander's chapter provides a synopsis of how different countries have decentralized their hospital sectors and reviews the key areas in which health-sector decentralization has affected hospitals. Several examples show the range of choices that countries can make in decentralizing their hospitals. Five main issues arise from these countries' experiences: (1) the role of hospitals relative to the other decentralized units, (2) control over hospital operations, (3) finances, (4) human resources, and (5) logistics. A detailed case study shows how hospital autonomy in Kenyatta National Hospital in Kenya has affected these areas. The chapter concludes with a discussion of three issues that should be anticipated when hospitals are being decentralized: the lack of capacity of many local managers and politicians to deal with the complexity of hospital management; the appropriateness of the degree to which hospitals are being decentralized; and the range of steps required to ensure that hospital autonomy furthers the goals of improved quality of care, efficiency, revenue generation, and greater accountability.

The anthology concludes with Robert Northrup's review of Indonesia's incremental progress toward decentralization over 23 years. The government health system in the 1970s was almost entirely centrally planned and managed. In the 1980s, the US Agency for International Development (USAID), intent on promoting a wider distribution of power, funded the Comprehensive Health Improvement Project—Province Specific (CHIPPS), whose goal was both to empower provinces in their negotiations with the center and to stimulate local responses to local needs. CHIPPS began the process of capacity development at the provincial level, which provided a critical base of experience in decentralized planning and management. This eventually led to the recognition by central leaders that some degree of decentralization was indeed beneficial. The subsequent series of World Bank–funded projects has been specifically aimed at decentralization. The center's commitment to decentralization was made clear in the most recent Health Project IV (HP-IV), which is directed at improving district-level planning and management. Although HP-IV has had an observable impact in these two areas, the old pattern of waiting for direction from above has not completely disappeared. Northrup's conclusion from his Indonesia experience is that peripheral capacity development; pilot efforts in better data collection, analysis, and use; and gradual accumulation of experience at both central and peripheral management levels are more likely to result in successful decentralization, without the chaotic transition period that many other countries have experienced.

PART I
Technical Support

Planning for and within Decentralized Health Systems

Malcolm Bryant

DECENTRALIZATION HAS BECOME extremely popular during the last decade. There are few nations, states, or provinces that remain untouched by it. There is a solid body of knowledge and experience to guide planners faced with or contemplating the decentralization of health services. It is therefore surprising to find that in many circumstances decentralization continues to be poorly planned and ineffectively implemented, and its impact on health status and service delivery poorly evaluated or understood.

Decentralization is a political and administrative process that may bring many benefits by stimulating improved efficiency and effectiveness of health services delivery. It offers the opportunity to empower individuals to take more responsibility for improving their own health and the health status of their community. Decentralization is also an extremely complicated, convoluted, and misunderstood process that may be entered into for a variety of reasons. It may be an attempt by leaders to restore equity to a system that no longer represents all the stakeholders, the result of local communities' effecting a revolutionary "grab" for control over their own lives, or a last-ditch effort by desperate politicians struggling to deal with falling standards and out-of-control costs. In each case, decentralization has come to be viewed as an almost magical solution to the problems that beset the health care system.

Planners are often not given the opportunity to provide input into the decision to decentralize, nor do they have sufficient information after the decision is made to understand the process they are engaged in. For these reasons, many avoidable mistakes are made. These retard the process, squander considerable political capital, and result in a worsening of the state of health services.

Planners must understand the key elements of decentralization, identify its benefits and drawbacks in their local situation, and apply sound planning principles to the process. This chapter attempts to remove some of the air of mystery that has grown up around decentralization by providing planners with the tools necessary to avoid the most common pitfalls and unnecessary mistakes.

Conceiving Decentralization

Politicians make the decisions about the nature of decentralization, the degree of authority decentralized, the roles of the public and private sectors, and the speed with which decentralization will take place. These decisions may be driven by a variety of internal (political) or external (donor-related) factors. The health sector has traditionally not played a strong role in shaping the political process, and this is certainly true for decentralization policy. This situation is unfortunate, because it is at this level that many preventable errors occur. Health planners and senior staff need to make themselves aware of the issues raised by decentralization, the local health situation, and the political imperatives. They must use this information to actively engage with the process through advocacy and lobbying. In this way, they can influence the development of decentralization policy and set the framework in a more appropriate fashion for effective implementation.

Some of the common, avoidable problems that have been observed as a result of decentralization include (1):

- fragmentation of health services
- inequity of the health sector compared with other sectors

- rent-seeking behavior (2) shifted downward and the development of local hierarchies
- a weakening of the central Ministry of Health to the point of nonfunctionality
- development of poor public health policy because local desires are not in line with public health goals

Table 1.1 lists some important benefits and drawbacks from decentralization, observed from case studies in several different countries. (3)

Decentralization must be shaped to improve both the functioning of the health system and the health and welfare of the population to be served. Health planners must educate themselves about the issues and become both advocates and lobbyists if they are to effectively shape this process.

Planning for Decentralization

Once the decision to decentralize is made and the framework defined, the planner's role is to plan implementation of the policy in a cost-effective and efficient manner. In an ideal world, decentralization policy would be well defined, appropriately targeted to the local situation and needs, and guaranteed to bring about the desired goals. In the real world, the policy is often flawed, but good planners can prevent poor policy formulation from being converted into bad implementation.

The group responsible for planning to implement decentralization encompasses economists, financial planners, lawyers, political scientists, and human resources experts, with health planners in the minority. This group's key challenge is to facilitate the shift from central-level control to central-peripheral partnership and help transfer authority and accountability to the periphery. If this is to go smoothly, the peripheral levels must be involved early in the process.

Planning a decentralized system is a confusing experience. A consistent planning approach is necessary to minimize the confusion.

Table 1.1 Potential Benefits and Drawbacks of Decentralization

Activity	Benefits	Drawbacks
Strategic planning	Greater emphasis can be placed on strategic planning and program performance	Local ownership or control of the program can conflict with leadership from the central level
Decision making	Local decisions can be made more quickly with fewer bureaucratic restrictions and are usually more relevant to regional or local needs	Local decisions may not support national program goals; decisions may be strongly influenced by local politics
Coordination	Central level can pay more attention to improving intersectoral coordination and collaboration at all levels	Too many organizations working at the local level can make coordination unmanageable
Local participation	Local-level service providers can participate in the program and coordinate their programs	Local participants may divert program activities from national goals
Performance planning	Local staff can establish performance objectives and be held accountable for meeting those objectives	Local objectives may not be consistent with national program goals
Financial sustainability	Central management level is compelled to address the issue of financial sustainability of individual health programs as it reduces subsidization of these programs	Less money may be available for implementing the program, which can worsen regional and local inequities and compromise quality and availability of services
Financial management	Program coverage can be expanded, and local revenue generation can be increased	Local-level staff may not have the skills to manage finances, and/or funds may be misused
Resource use	Determination of resources needed for health services, logistics, supervision, information, education, and communication can be more appropriate	Central level may not agree with local priorities and may not be willing to finance local initiatives
Staffing	Staff recruitment can be done at the local level and within the communities served by the program	Local loyalties and affiliations may inappropriately influence the selection and promotion of staff
Supervision	Supervision can be directly linked to and influence planning at the local level	Weak supervisory skills may result in mistakes in applying national standards of care
Service standards	Central level can focus on national issues such as service standards and norms and program evaluation criteria	National service standards and norms may be inappropriate or nonimplementable at the local level
Client satisfaction	Services can be more easily integrated or coordinated and better organized to meet client needs and convenience	Referral systems may break down, and outreach activities may be cut if the local government does not have sufficient funds to cover transportation costs
New services	Opportunities are greater for developing new or innovative services or service delivery mechanisms	Inadequate local planning capacities or lack of vision may lead to unrealistic service delivery objectives and strategies

Source: Riitta-Liisa Kolehmainen-Aitken and William Newbrander, *Decentralizing the management of health and family planning programs*, Lessons from FPMD series (Boston: Management Sciences for Health, 1997).

There is no definitive "right way" to plan for decentralization, but the experience of working in many countries (4) suggests that the approach outlined below may be of value.

Motivating Forces

Understanding the complex web of motivations is essential. The health planner may not be able to significantly influence these motivating forces, but knowing why a policy is being developed is important. It facilitates long-term planning and enables both the alignment of the goals and objectives with expectations and the construction of an important implementation framework. For example, the plans developed for a government that is decentralizing to improve the health of its rural people may differ from the plans of a government decentralizing as a result of pressure from external forces in order to secure a desperately needed loan.

Opposing Forces and Obstacles

It is important to know what forces are opposing decentralization so that they can be considered as plans are developed. These forces include:

- unrealistic expectations
- reluctance of central-level authorities to give up control
- lack of trust in the central authority by local levels
- competition between the health sector and other sectors
- lack of public engagement in the process
- failure to take into account the true costs of decentralization
- organized opposition (e.g., unions, civil servants)
- failure to allocate adequate resources at the peripheral levels
- lack of a supporting legal framework

Goals and Objectives

Goals and objectives may be either explicit or implicit. Both types of goals must be understood if a new health service is to be planned effectively. Planners must establish a realistic set of expectations of both themselves and the system being reformed. It is important to avoid the situation in which, after many months or years, someone can step back and ask, "Are we there yet?" only to find that you do not know where "there" is.

Functional Definitions

It is important to know what decentralization means in the specific context. Decentralization is a process, not a state of being, and it does not have a uniform and unambiguous definition. The planner must define the process, identify the areas of ambiguity, and articulate what is meant by the various commonly used terms in the particular setting.

Legal Framework

Transferring power frequently requires changing legal frameworks. Decentralization requires new legislation, and these new laws need to be studied carefully. Existing laws and regulations also need to be reviewed to determine whether they are contradictory to or unsupportive of decentralization and thus should be repealed or rewritten. In addition, new regulations may need to be developed. Special care must be paid to making sure that the legal framework does not turn health care workers into "lawbreakers."

Management Systems

Decentralization does not fix bad management. Decentralization places new demands on existing management systems such as planning; financial management and budgeting; human resources management (including training); logistics systems for vehicles, equipment, and medications; and management information systems. To ensure that each system functions optimally, planners must define the roles and responsibilities at each level, determine the critical linkages between levels, and establish the linkages to other sectors.

Financial and Human Resources Costs

It is often stated that decentralization reduces costs by decreasing bureaucracy, but there is no evidence to support this statement. In fact, the more devolution of power and authority that takes place, the higher the level of effort required, which implies the potential for *increased* costs. Peripheral management systems need to be established, and staff need to be redeployed or new staff hired. Health professionals, managers, and board and community members must be trained, and elections may need to be held. These are not simply one-time investment costs but will require continual input and recurrent cost expenditures. Planners must quantify these costs and accurately predict both the capital costs and the recurrent costs associated with decentralization in their particular setting.

Phase-in and Implementation

Decentralization does not have to be introduced all at once. It is reasonable (and often desirable) to introduce it in a stepwise, logical fashion, allowing lessons learned from practice to direct the next step forward. If overwhelming change takes place too suddenly, it is likely to draw opposition. The same magnitude of change taking place in small, controlled steps over an extended period can create confidence, reduce anxiety, and present an opportunity to learn and adapt. Phasing in can be organized by level, by function, or by service.

Skills Development

Many people in the newly decentralized system will lack some of the skills required. Health care providers must become managers. Community members must take on governance roles. Local administrators need to understand health imperatives. All the participants need to be given the appropriate skills to do their new jobs, and they must have those skills before they take responsibility for their new roles.

An inventory of skills and the transfer and redeployment of staff to distribute existing skills are important first steps. Remaining deficits can then be corrected by carefully targeted training and hiring of new staff.

Communications

An important factor in managing change is good communication. Individuals can accept delays, failures, and complications much better if they know what is going on, why it is happening, and how they are going to be affected personally. Failure to address this issue will result in a loss of morale, generate resentment, and set the stage for conflict. Clear communication channels to health care providers, managers, local authorities, local politicians, and community members need to be established so that each group can be actively engaged. In addition, forums need to be available where staff and community can raise their concerns, feedback mechanisms need to be created, and specific procedures must be developed to resolve conflicts as and when they arise.

Monitoring, Evaluation, and Refinement

The planner must ensure that one of the first systems established is the monitoring and adjustment of the decentralization process itself. Baseline studies need to be designed and conducted; clear, unambiguous indicators of progress need to be defined; and a schedule for measuring indicators has to be set.

Health Planning Roles under Decentralization

In many circumstances, planning has been an annual or quinquennial activity, leading to the production of detailed plans that were widely distributed, filed, and rarely (if ever) consulted again. Planners have been centrally located and isolated from implementation of the plans they developed. Planning has been a linear process whose sole purpose was the production of a plan. The response has been to broaden the planning process to include stakeholders from throughout the system and to link planners to those responsible for implementing plans. The linear process has become a planning cycle. This, in turn, has led to health plans that are more realistic and more likely to be carried out and have local support. (5)

Decentralization represents another important step forward. It offers the potential to transfer authority and accountability from the central level to the peripheral level. Unfortunately, experience has shown a mixed success rate in effecting this transfer. Too often roles have been inadequately delineated, responsibility poorly communicated, and accountability transferred without authority. The result has often been the failure of plans and the passing of blame from one level to another.

For decentralization to be effective, it must permanently change the relationship between planners at the central and peripheral levels. Although there is no "right answer" to how the planning process should proceed in a decentralized setting, a measure of authority, responsibility, and accountability must pass to the periphery and must be matched by a commensurate release of control at the central level.

Individuals and ministries can find a decentralized planning process difficult and threatening. Several factors also impede the process:

- It is a much slower process when there is wide stakeholder involvement.
- It requires more effort to involve the periphery.
- For coherent peripheral input, time and effort must be invested in training peripheral stakeholders.
- Coordinating input from a wide range of peripheral sources is difficult and requires skills that health planners do not necessarily have.
- Inputs from the periphery may be contrary to central-level needs, which creates a tension between listening to and acting on peripheral input. (1)

The Role of the Central Level in Decentralized Planning

Central-level planners must:

- make demographic projections and epidemiological analyses and use them to set long-range goals and strategies for the national health and population programs
- establish national goals for improving the health status of different population groups
- with the involvement of local-level managers, formulate a national strategic plan that uses research and survey data, is based on realistic objectives, and can be implemented at the local level
- determine program performance standards to achieve national goals

In a centralized system, planners are usually full-time workers who can draw on a wide range of specialist resources. In a decentralized system, planners already have jobs as managers or health care providers and work as planners only part-time. They have little or no formal training in planning and almost no access to technical resources. The primary role of the central-level planner must change from that of a detached expert to that of an enabler, mentor, teacher, and technical assistant to staff at the peripheral level.

Central-level planners should perform a second role as coordinators of peripheral plans, drawing these plans together into a "national" plan. The central planners will develop their own plans targeted to those activities needed to bring the peripheral plans to fruition. When cuts or changes must be made because of resource limitations or the need to follow national standards, clear communication, negotiation, and consensus must be sought. In many circumstances, well-meaning central-level officials eliminate priority areas from plans, set new priority areas, and make seemingly arbitrary decisions about what will and will not be funded. As a result, staff in the periphery suffer a sense of disempowerment and may disengage from the process.

The third role of central-level planners is to anticipate the inevitable rise of forces that will oppose decentralization and to coordinate efforts to counter those forces before they derail the process. Anticipating political changes, working with professional organizations and labor unions, mediating between government divisions that may fear loss of control, and coordinating with donors who often emphasize vertical programming become vital.

The Role of the Peripheral Level in Decentralized Planning

Local-level managers must:

- develop operational plans and manage integrated services
- analyze clients and services and know how to use that information to make program improvements
- set program targets for catchment areas that are consistent with national goals
- create conditions that encourage community members to participate in planning and implementing the local health program

The primary role of the peripheral level is to develop locally appropriate strategic and implementation plans to achieve local and national goals. Local-level planners must understand the constraints that the central level faces and must also know the extent of their own freedom and control. Continued, strong engagement of peripheral staff in the process is crucial, and great care must be taken to establish communication channels that enable this. Without this communication and trust, peripheral planners will quickly become disempowered, lose motivation, and disengage from the process. The result will be a failure of the decentralization process.

Guidelines to Help Health Planners Introduce Decentralization

The theoretical and analytical information presented above, the case studies and surveys it is drawn from, and the practical lessons learned are important to understanding the process of decentralization.

However, the average practitioner rarely consults a textbook when addressing a frequently encountered problem. He or she tends to rely on short lists and mnemonics to remember critical steps and decision points. A planner confronted with decentralization may find the following guidelines useful. These steps are not comprehensive, they are not definitive, and they are not guaranteed to produce successful plans if followed. However, they remove some of the mystique that continues to surround decentralization and can help put health planners back in control of their own environment.

Action Is Vital

DO SOMETHING, TAKE THE LEAD, DO NOT BE PASSIVE. Many health managers who have worked in a centralized system are used to someone else deciding for them. Decentralization *should* bring an end to that, but breaking the habit of waiting to be told what to do is hard.

BE FLEXIBLE AND DO NOT BE AFRAID TO BACKTRACK. If you acknowledge that decentralization is the politician's agenda and not yours, it will be easier to accept that you are not, and never will be, in control. Things will change around you, and you need to be flexible enough to change with them and to accept that sometimes the directions you have set up will be reversed or changed. Rigidity and inflexibility will ultimately lead to conflict and failure.

BE PREPARED TO DEFEND YOURSELF, BUT DO NOT BE DEFENSIVE. Planning and leading a process as complicated as decentralization requires that you believe in what you are doing. Because there is no "right" way to do things, there will be detractors and critics. The best way to defend against these critics is to be armed with good information, have a clear vision of what you are going to achieve, and communicate that vision.

BE PREPARED TO TAKE RISKS. Avoiding risk is comfortable, but effective reform cannot take place without challenging existing structures and conventional wisdom. Careful study and analysis can show the best way forward, but innovation and systematic improvements cannot take place without a willingness to risk failure. This should not become an excuse for reckless behavior, however.

Good, Appropriate Information Is the Only Way Forward

BE PREPARED WITH GOOD INFORMATION. The step of gathering good data cannot be omitted if you are to have compelling information to support your approach and convince health workers, politicians, and community members of the value of change. Most importantly, such data will provide a baseline against which you can measure change (positive or negative) as you implement your plans.

BASE PROGRAM MANAGEMENT ON SOUND INFORMATION. Demographic, health, political, and service delivery statistics are critical to setting up any program, but ongoing monitoring and evaluation must generate information that will guide the implementation of the program.

Do Not Try to Do Things Alone

SEEK ASSISTANCE OFTEN AND FROM PEOPLE WHO CAN HELP. Do not be too proud. You cannot know everything. You will need the participation of people with similar experience.

FIND AND SUPPORT COMMITTED LEADERS. Seek out influential leaders who can lend weight to the changes you want to make. Use their support to overcome opposition and public criticism.

DEVELOP A CRITICAL MASS OF COMMITTED MANAGERS. As you work to change a system, make sure that you have enough managers who understand the changes and can support them. Many will be unwilling or unable to understand what you are trying to do, and opposition within the system can be fierce. Do not try to overcome this opposition alone.

LOOK FOR ALLIES IN THE HEALTH SECTOR AND ELSEWHERE. Even if other sectors are not decentralizing, they will be affected by what you are doing. It is important that staff in other sectors become allies rather than competitors or detractors.

Understand What You Are Doing, and Communicate It to Others

BE CLEAR IN YOUR OWN MIND WHAT YOU ARE DOING. Understand what decentralization is all about and what your role is. Are you simply following a political agenda that is being thrust on you? Are you doing it because you will lose your job if you refuse? Do you believe that decentralization is the single most important step to improve the health of the people in your country?

BE HONEST WITH OTHERS ABOUT WHAT YOU ARE DOING. If you are decentralizing to save money, be prepared to say so. Do not insult people's intelligence by saying that decentralization is designed to improve services. People may not like the truth, but they like deception even less. This applies to both health staff and the general population.

KNOW WHAT IS LEGAL AND WHAT IS NOT. If legal changes need to be made to implement your plans, identify them early. This means that you must know the legal framework for service delivery and understand how flexible it is. Plans that require health care providers to break the law will not work. Some laws can be changed, and others cannot. If the laws cannot be changed, you need a different plan.

INVOLVE THE COMMUNITY AT THE LOCAL LEVEL. Make sure that you know what community members want and need, and make sure that you have the mechanisms to communicate to them what you are actually doing.

DO NOT DISCOUNT THE IMPORTANCE OF LOCAL POLITICIANS. They can be neutral, they can be allies, or they can be against you, but they cannot be ignored.

Make Sure Your Priorities Are Right

FOCUS ON WHAT MATTERS. You cannot have a system without basic supports. Your data gathering and situational analysis should have identified the key issues. Make sure that you know what is critical, and ensure that it is addressed. For example, a system without essential drugs does not work, no matter how well everything else functions.

FOCUS ON WHAT IS ALREADY WORKING WELL AND MAKE IT STRONGER, AND TAKE WHAT IS NOT WORKING WELL AND REMOVE OR REFORM IT. Acknowledgment of these two elements and visible action may cost little but will make the process of change much smoother.

Prepare Your Colleagues and Coworkers

EDUCATE HEALTH WORKERS. Take the time to involve the health workers in the system. Do not just keep them informed; actively involve them in decision making.

EDUCATE THE POPULATION. As with health workers, inform and involve the community.

ENSURE THAT EVERYONE HAS THE NECESSARY TOOLS. Health workers need knowledge and skills to facilitate the process you are planning, and so does the community. You cannot demand that a community perform a needs assessment without providing it with the knowledge and tools to do so. To ignore this factor will waste time and resources and cause frustration. Invest the resources in making sure that people have the tools, expertise, and money required to do the basic tasks.

References

1. Ross, A. "Decentralization in the health sector in developing countries: Panacea or Pandora's box?" PowerPoint presentation. USAID and USPHS, 1997.
2. Rent-seeking behavior has been defined as "the expenditure of resources in order to bring about an uncompensated transfer of goods or services from another person or persons to one's self as the result of a 'favorable' decision on some public policy" (Felkins, L. 1997. "Rent-Seeking Behavior." In "A Rational Life: A Discussion of the Peculiar Consequences of Individuals Living in Groups" [home page]. [cited January 4, 1999]. Available from magnolia.net/~leonf/politics/ rentseek. html; INTERNET.)

3. Kolehmainen-Aitken, R. L., and W. Newbrander. *Decentralizing the management of health and family planning programs.* Lessons from FPMD Series. Boston: Management Sciences for Health, 1997, pp. 31–33.
4. Ibid., pp. 28–43.
5. Reinke, W. A. *Health planning for effective management.* New York: Oxford University Press, 1988.

2
Financing, Service Delivery, and Decentralization in the Philippines and Kenya

Charles C. Stover

FINANCING STRATEGIES CAN AFFECT health service delivery in many ways, as well as impact the pace and type of decentralization. This chapter compares the experiences of financial management under the devolution of health services in the Philippines on January 1, 1993, and those under the cost-sharing program in Kenya at the same time. The two experiences—one a complete devolution of responsibility for the health system to the local government unit (LGU) level, the other a mild form of financial decentralization—originated for different reasons and had different impacts at the time and afterward. The contrast illustrates how different financing strategies can either lead decentralization or follow it.

The experience in Kenya shows that the cost-sharing program (charging fees in public health facilities) paved the way for further decentralization of the health sector in the absence of a master plan or overall political consensus for decentralization. The steps necessary to administer the cost-sharing funds in a decentralized manner at the district level preceded steps to further decentralize administrative responsibility for health services. (1)

In sharp contrast, the experience in the Philippines shows how the devolution of health services caused significant changes in the fiscal systems in the health field. The costs of health services, as represented by physical assets of buildings and equipment and by

Figure 2.1 Cause and Effect in Decentralization

- **Kenya**
  Cost-sharing program paved the way for incremental decentralization

- **Philippines**
  Devolution caused massive shifts in the financing and delivery of health services

---

personnel, were transferred from the national Department of Health to the provinces and municipalities. Revenue to pay for health services was separated from these expenses and allocated according to a formula based on population and related factors. (2)

Kenya and the Philippines represent two ends of the spectrum of decentralization (Figure 2.1). These two examples illustrate that health financing, service delivery, and decentralization in the health sector are interrelated in complex yet different ways. Much of the information here is gained from the direct experience of the author. Management Sciences for Health managed two large bilateral projects with US Agency for International Development (USAID) support in both of these countries. (3)

Philippines Devolution

The delegation of financial responsibility and revenue-generating capabilities to local authorities often accompanies decentralization. The case in the Philippines is a dramatic example. Effective January 1, 1993, nearly all health programs in the Philippines, including 595 national government hospitals, were transferred to the LGUs, which consisted of 78 provinces and 1,543 municipalities. (4) Preparations over an 18-month period preceding the transfer included completing inventories of all buildings, equipment, and supplies, plus com-

Figure 2.2 Devolution in the Philippines

- Political decision that encompassed health services

- Transfer of 80–90% of government services:
  - 595 hospitals
  - 12,859 rural health units, municipal health centers, and *barangay* health stations
  - Most public health programs

- Transfer of health personnel, equipment, and assets

- Effective January 1993, after 18 months of lead time

piling detailed rosters of personnel. The transfer included all personnel, facilities, equipment, and other assets of the Department of Health, except those specifically designated to remain part of the national government (Figure 2.2). Personnel who were not accepted by the local government remained with the national government until their cases could be adjudicated.

The devolution was mandated as part of legislation designed to permanently diminish the role of the national government ("Imperial Manila") in the post-Marcos period. The political motivation was to make health and other services more responsive to local governments and populations. The Local Government Code (Republic Act No. 7160) devolved a wide range of powers over health services, social welfare and development, environment and natural resources, and tourism to LGUs. Powers held by the Department of Education were not included in the law, presumably as a result of strong lobbying by teachers' organizations. The provincial and municipal governments were already well established but had not previously had responsibility for health services, except for some public health programs and a number of municipal hospitals.

The Department of Health resisted the devolution until about one year before implementation, at which point senior management accepted the decision and worked to help ensure a smooth implementation. Devolution created major problems for the health sector, since vertical programs such as immunization were split; career health personnel were removed from the national service and transferred to municipal and provincial service, often at lower pay scales; and the national drug procurement service was replaced by a different system in each LGU. The major line responsibilities of the national Department of Health were replaced by ill-defined mandates to establish health policy and set standards. The regional offices of the department were left with a limited set of responsibilities, often defined as part of the remaining functions of the national department.

The public financing of health services changed dramatically as well (Figure 2.3). The costs of devolved health services became the responsibility of the LGUs. Revenue for these services was allocated on a formula basis independent of their costs. The formula used to allocate national revenue to LGUs took into account demographics and, to some extent, poverty, but not the existing distribution of health facilities and programs. Thus, health service costs and national revenue entered into the LGU budgets as unrelated items.

As a result of the financing changes, there was a considerable gap between the costs of personnel and facilities devolved to provinces and the national revenue allocated at the provincial level. Municipalities often fared better in terms of the balance of revenue and devolved expenses. In the provinces, deficits in the health sector had to be addressed, along with demands for other provincial services. Prior national policies of offering free services were often amended, and cutbacks were made in the funding of health services. The financing systems, both public and private (such as insurance), had to respond to the dramatic changes driven by the political imperative to fundamentally restructure the government.

Creative thinking resulted in many initiatives to respond to the funding crisis. Several provinces developed voluntary health insurance schemes, which were marketed to residents to serve as a pooled funding source for both public and private health services. (5), (6) In effect, the old national mold was shattered, and many new forms of financing and organizing health services evolved—some better and some worse than those that existed previously.

Figure 2.3 Fiscal Impact of Devolution in the Philippines

- Public financing of health services included in comprehensive revenue allocation

- Formula driven by demographics, but not by cost of health sevices devolved

- Major impact on financial and delivery systems

- At provincial level, deficit addressed by:
  - Cost reductions
  - Fee increases
  - New revenue sources, e.g., provincial health insurance schemes

In addition, new policies and procedures were developed rapidly. For example, in many provinces, drug procurement for public hospitals was initially incorporated into the regular procedures for procurement of other goods and services. As a result, procurement was delayed by the multiple signatures required. One province even used a courier to expedite the paperwork from one office to another. Procedures were eventually streamlined, but the breakdown of the national drug procurement system was a casualty of the devolution.

Kenya Cost-Sharing Program

The situation in Kenya was considerably different (Figure 2.4). There, the starting point for decentralization was the cost-sharing program in the Ministry of Health (MOH). There was no sustained debate and no decision regarding decentralization of health and other services—no political mandate. During the 1980s, Kenya suffered a deepening economic crisis in terms of slow or negative economic growth, inflation, and continued high population growth. As a result, recurrent per capita expenditures of the MOH fell from

Figure 2.4 Cost-Sharing in Kenya

- No political mandate for decentralization

- Slow economic growth caused crisis in government funding for health services

- Drop in per capita government spending for health from $7.56 in FY 1979–80 to $4.60 in FY 1991–92

- Cost-sharing program part of health reform program

- District Health Management Boards managed cost-sharing revenue for locally agreed-on improvements

- Additional revenue raised from fees and insurance collections:
  - 6–13% of total budget
  - 20–37% of nonpersonnel budget

- Efficiency improved through differential fee structure with waivers and exemptions

---

$7.56 in fiscal year (FY) 1979–80 to $4.60 in FY 1991–92 in constant US dollar terms. The 1989–93 Health Policy Reform, linked in part to the structural adjustment program, included the introduction of cost-sharing for government health services.

Inpatient and outpatient fees were first initiated in December 1989 without adequate preparation of the public, and the cost-sharing program faced political opposition. Patients were upset when government facilities charged a consultation fee even when there were no drugs in stock. Since little background education had been done, the public did not understand that the purpose of the fees was to generate revenue to improve services. The President rescinded outpatient fees in September 1990 as the last of many changes to reduce the impact of the unpopular program.

The program was reimplemented on a phased basis with careful preparation and training starting in June 1991 and extending through July 1993. A public education campaign preceded the relaunching of the program. Fees were charged for drugs but not for consultations, which was more politically acceptable. Above all, the program was established on a decentralized footing at the district level. District Health Management Boards were appointed by the President, with the authority and responsibility to collect, account for, and spend revenue from the cost-sharing program for locally agreed-upon service improvements.

Based on the program design principles, the cost-sharing program was established at the level of the health facility, with a primary focus at the district level (district hospitals and health centers). Health dispensaries were exempted from the fee system. Revenue was to be retained at the facility level, not recaptured by the Ministry of Finance. Further, the funds would be "additive and without year"; the Ministry would not decrease funding based on collections, and the funds could be spent after the close of the fiscal year. The funds would be spent for improvements in both curative treatment (75 percent) and primary health care (25 percent) through local processes of priority setting, with flexibility to meet local needs. Through local involvement in decision making, the community could see improvements in services as a result of the fee collection, which strengthened support for the program.

Thus, decentralized financial systems and decision making were the first initiatives toward decentralization of health services in Kenya. Personnel were still hired and assigned through the national MOH, drugs were purchased and distributed through the MOH, and budgets were determined through the national process. The cost-sharing revenue was the only locally controlled funding and often the only discretionary, flexible funding available to meet unmet needs. Where the cost-sharing program has worked effectively, the service improvements funded by the program are visible. In other areas where the program has not worked effectively or has not been properly controlled, there is little visible impact.

After relaunching on a phased basis, the program has continued to make significant improvements in the financing and quality of health services. The funds collected average 6 to 13 percent of total budgeted costs and 20 to 37 percent of nonpersonnel expenditures, depending on the type of facility. (1)

Besides raising additional revenue through patient fees and collections from the National Hospital Insurance Fund to improve health services, the program was designed to achieve other efficiency objectives. By charging nominal fees for services at hospitals and health centers (but not dispensaries), the program was designed to reduce unnecessary visits. Differential fees (higher at provincial hospitals) were set to encourage more rational referral patterns. To ensure equity in access, waivers based on ability to pay were designed to protect the poor, and exemptions for certain groups, such as children under the age of five, were implemented.

Although these waivers and exemptions were important, they were not always implemented appropriately. Some people who could not afford to pay were not granted waivers. The inherent inequity of people living in richer provinces being able to afford to pay more in fees was not corrected by the program, since revenues were retained locally and not redistributed. However, a uniform national fee schedule did help avoid more extreme regional differences. Many of these issues have been studied to help improve operation of the system. (7)

After the policy decisions for the cost-sharing program were made, the lack of ability at the local level to handle the administration of the program created many difficulties and challenges. As discussed earlier, many parts of the first round of the program were halted within the first year and reimplemented after the development of systems and procedures, control and reporting mechanisms, and massive training initiatives.

After five years, many district boards have developed a track record of good performance and are expected to receive additional responsibilities under the various options for decentralization being considered by the Ministry. Other boards, not surprisingly, have had mixed or poor reviews. Overall, the experience of creating district boards and involving the community in the use of cost-sharing funds to improve health services has provided a model for increased decentralization. The systems and procedures for managing cost-sharing funds can also become the basis for expanded systems, should the current proposals for block grants to selected districts be implemented.

Table 2.1 Starting or Ending Point?

Philippines	Kenya
Rapid devolution	Gradual development of financial systems under cost sharing
Financial systems followed changes	Development of limited decision making at district level
Difficult or impossible to reverse	Successful models for further decentralization
Creative financing solutions	Gradualist approach—no overriding policy for decentralization
	Ongoing debate about further decentralization

In summary, although the cost-sharing program started without any specific policy intention of leading to decentralization, it has evolved into the basic infrastructure for additional decentralization. This process of capacity building is slow and deliberate and is subject to setbacks due to turnover of personnel. But it also provides an important contrast to the more extreme and rapidly executed devolution in the Philippines (Table 2.1).

Continuing Change

Starting in the spring of 1997, partially in preparation for the national elections, the Government of Kenya showed renewed interest in decentralizing health services as a means of improving quality through local participation. Hospital boards for provincial and district hospitals were appointed, though without clear guidelines for their roles and responsibilities. Many district and provincial boards are starting to use their general management mandates and the specific financial systems under the cost-sharing program to assert themselves to improve services. Attempts are under way to clarify the implications of decentralization and to formulate clear policies regarding the Ministry's and the Government's strategy on decentralization. (8), (9), (10) Perhaps a resolution will come when these local initiatives take sufficient hold that they challenge prevailing national policies in personnel and budgeting.

An important related issue is hospital autonomy. Several government announcements have stated the policy objective of granting provincial hospitals autonomous status, along the lines of the successful precedent set by Kenyatta National Hospital. (10) Policy documents are being prepared as part of the ongoing debate. Although there are high-level policy statements in favor of autonomy, it is not clear where the impetus for the change is coming from or what the overall government position on this issue is. Meanwhile, donor-funded projects are exploring the feasibility of hospital autonomy, as well as block grants, as ways to stimulate better management and improve services. Many of the specific proposals build on the financial and resource management systems developed under the cost-sharing program. These policies, procedures, and systems can be an important core element for further decentralization, once the political debate about decentralization of health services is resolved. In any case, the situation is fluid, with great room for improvement in services if the right combination of leadership and resources can be mobilized within the prevailing legal and policy constraints.

Meanwhile, in the Philippines, the struggle to adapt to new circumstances in financing and managing health services continues. Many creative solutions are being implemented at the provincial and municipal levels, and the national Department of Health is recasting itself as a planning, standard-setting, and regulatory agency for both public and private sectors. It is impossible to tell whether the health system is working better as a result of devolution. What is certain is that the political objective of breaking the central "Imperial Manila" syndrome has been achieved.

References

1. Collins, D. C., et al. *Health financing reform in Kenya: The fall and rise of cost sharing, 1989–94.* Boston: Management Sciences for Health, 1996.
2. Taylor, R., et al. *End-of-project evaluation of the Philippines Health Finance Development Project.* Arlington, VA: TvT Associates, 1997.

3. Kenya Health Financing Project under USAID contract 623-0245-C-00-0040 and Philippines Health Finance Development Project under USAID contract 492-0446-C-00-2114-00.
4. Pérez, J. M. C. Alfiler, and M. Victoriano, *Managing transition dilemmas in the early years of devolution in the Philippines*. Decentralization and Health Systems Change Project. Geneva: WHO; Manila: Department of Health, October 1995.
5. Palisoc, A. *Bukidnon health insurance project—Manual of operations*, version I. Philippines Health Finance Development Project. Management Sciences for Health. USAID Contract No. 492-0446-C-00-2114-00. June 1994.
6. Palisoc, A. *Tarlac health maintenance program system and procedures manual*, vol. 1. Philippines Health Finance Development Project. Management Sciences for Health. USAID Contract No. 492-0446-C-00-2114-00. December 1994.
7. Newbrander, W. *Equity in the provision of health care: Ensuring access of the poor to services under user fee systems*. Washington, DC: BASICS Project, 1995.
8. Fox, J. *Health sector decentralisation: A Kenyan framework*. AFS Project. Management Sciences for Health. USAID Contract No. 623-0264-C-00-7005. May 1997.
9. Fox, J. *Health sector decentralisation in Kenya: A consideration of key issues*. AFS Project. Management Sciences for Health. USAID Contract No. 623-0264-C-00-7005. June 1997.
10. Collins, D., G. Njeru, and J. Meme. *Hospital autonomy: The experience of Kenyatta National Hospital*. Management Sciences for Health. Data for Decision-Making Project. USAID Cooperative Agreement DPE-5991-A-00-1052-00. June 1996.

3
Human Resources Development under Decentralization

Riitta-Liisa Kolehmainen-Aitken

DECENTRALIZATION OF POLITICAL and administrative power is becoming an increasingly prevalent component of health-sector reform in all parts of the world, from Asia to Africa, from Europe to South America. This transfer of power away from the center is often combined with an effort to reform an outdated and cumbersome civil service structure. These reform processes are particularly prevalent in countries under structural adjustment, where funding agencies such as the World Bank are important partners in the process of reform and, in many instances, its driving force. Yet the wider implications of decentralization for human resources planning, training, and management (jointly referred to as human resources development in this chapter) are generally poorly researched and inadequately understood.

Human resources are the most important component of the health care system for converting available pharmaceuticals, medical technology, and preventive health information into better health for a nation. Training young people to become skilled health workers takes a long time, and the cost of employing them once they are trained is high. In most countries, salaries and benefits consume up to three-quarters of the recurrent health budget. For these reasons, human resources considerations should command a great deal of attention in any decentralization discussion. That this is frequently not the case reflects both the general inattention to human resources issues (other than training) that prevails in many countries and the conceptual vagueness of "decentralization."

"Decentralization" is a term that continues to be used to describe a wide variety of power-sharing arrangements. (1) It can signify the transfer of limited administrative responsibility from a central Ministry of Health to local health offices, or it can involve the creation of new governmental structures, such as provincial governments, that are responsible for providing health and many other services. The implications of decentralization for human resources are greatly influenced by the degree to which political and/or administrative power is transferred, how the new roles are defined, what skills are available at the local level, and what administrative linkages exist between the different management levels and between the central health authority and the other central government offices that influence resource allocation (such as ministries of finance and civil service). Finally, they are also influenced by the degree of political will to make decentralization work.

A variety of political and economic reasons can influence a country to transfer power away from a central level. In recent years, however, decentralization has often been implemented as an integral component of health-sector reform. (2) Health-sector reform aims to improve the performance of the sector and, ultimately, the health of the people through a conscious process of setting sectoral priorities and policies and then reforming the way health services are structured and financed to fit with those revised priorities and policies. The consequent changes in organizational structures and institutions, such as national ministries of health or the civil service, have fundamental human resources implications. The success of health-sector reform in reaching its laudable goals thus depends on the amount of thought and preparation that human resources issues have been given.

This chapter analyzes the impact of decentralization on sound human resources development, based on the experience of the author and her colleagues at Management Sciences for Health and on the published literature. The findings come mainly, but not exclusively, from countries where decentralization has taken the form of devolution, that is, where both the decentralized activities and the staff performing them have been transferred substantially outside the central government's direct control. The most glaring problems tend to surface in these countries, and the text gives many examples of how decentralization has jeopardized important aspects of human resources development. This should not, however, lead to the conclusion that centralization of power would necessarily be a better option. Rather, these negative examples are presented to highlight the importance of considering human resources implications at every step of the decentralization process.

The chapter is divided into three sections. The first section looks at human resources issues that emerge as part of the process of transferring power to lower management levels. The second section focuses on identifying the human resources domains where problems arise as a result of the way decentralized management systems are structured. The third section provides recommendations for health leaders who are considering decentralizing or implementing reforms.

Before the Fact: Human Resources and the Decentralization Process

The decision to decentralize frequently arises outside the health sector and for reasons that have little to do with improving a nation's health. Political considerations are particularly prominent in countries that devolve substantial control over health services to local governments. Such devolution usually also encompasses the transfer of control over peripheral health staff from central to local authorities. The timetable for implementing these new arrangements is often constrained, allowing little time for examining the human resources implications of proposed reforms.

The politically highly charged decisions about new roles and responsibilities under devolution must be followed by the definition of new organizational structures and of terms and conditions of service at both the central and peripheral levels, and by the reallocation of staff between these two levels. Four important human resources issues emerge in this process:

1. the adequacy of available information on human resources
2. the complexity of transferring human resources
3. the impact of professional associations, unions, and registration bodies on the design and implementation of management structures and jobs
4. the morale and motivation of health staff

Adequacy of Available Information

Decisions on human resources will be sound only if they are based on appropriate and timely information. (3) Easy access to reliable data on staff is thus crucial to any decision about personnel allocation. This is true of a country that decides to maintain a single public service structure, as was done in Papua New Guinea, where in the 1980s each province was formed into a public service department to which members of the national public service were assigned full-time. (4) It is equally true of a country where members of the national public service become part of local government staff establishments, as in the Philippines. (5)

Basic personnel data, such as a health worker's name, professional qualifications, and age, are more likely to be available at the central level than is up-to-date, accurate information on the type and level of position held. Ministry of health or public services commission records on staff positions and the individuals holding them are notoriously flawed and out-of-date; salary data may be more reliable. Data on lower-level staff, particularly if they are not considered part of the public service, are often missing. Even when data are available, considerable time may be needed to verify their accuracy and completeness. Data on training intakes and outputs are often incomplete and inaccurate, since they come from multiple sources with different schedules of updating and standards of quality control.

Reilly's observations of the situation in Papua New Guinea at the time of decentralization are not unusual:

It was not possible to construct complete organizational structures for each health division of every province because of poor records kept at the Department of Health. The section of the Department which dealt with staffing did not know what positions were available in provinces or who filled them. . . . A similar problem was found with duty statements, which were out of date and not specific to the tasks to be performed. (6)

Complexity of Transferring Human Resources

The transfer of human resources to local control is a far more complex process than the handover of facilities or equipment. The following issues illustrate the range of decisions that need to be made:

- modifying or creating new organizational structures and positions at the central and local levels, and specifying the linkages between them
- revising job descriptions and reporting relationships
- defining new processes for personnel management
- deciding how to reallocate existing staff to new organizational structures
- transferring personnel records and staff
- mediating if the new employer refuses to accept the transfer
- dealing with individual staff members who will not or cannot transfer

First, decentralization calls for changes in the way human resources are organized into functional health care structures and in the jobs that staff perform. Organizational structures and positions at both central and local levels require modification to conform to the new division of powers and resource allocation patterns. Existing jobs may need to be redesigned, job descriptions revised, and reporting relationships amended to ensure the availability of the right combinations of skills in the new organizational structures. Terms and conditions of service may have to be altered to fit available resources.

Shaping the postdecentralization pattern of employment in the health sector through organizational design and job reprofiling is highly complex on a technical and operational level. It is also an intensely political and bureaucratic process that involves a variety of institutional actors, from health managers and professional associations to government officials and politicians. The differences in prior salary levels and conditions of service make this process particularly challenging in countries such as South Africa, where separate health delivery systems were combined under a new decentralized health care structure. (7)

The form that the new organizational structures take can be greatly influenced by central government decisions that emanate from outside the health sector. A stringent target for staff reduction may become their key determinant if decentralization occurs as a component of a national effort to reform the civil service. Cutting staff strength without considering the larger strategic implications for health care delivery may result in an organizational structure and staffing levels that are detrimental to important components of the health service. In Nepal, for example, the initial cuts at the central level paralyzed essential functions, such as the Expanded Programme on Immunization. (8)

Molding old organizational structures to suit the needs of decentralized management or creating new structures may be hindered by a strong agency in charge of the national civil service. In Papua New Guinea, it took a year to convince the Public Services Commission of the need to create administrator posts in the provincial health structures and another two years before these posts were advertised. (6) In the Philippines, a new Department of Health (DOH) organogram, which was developed with the help of outside consultants, was declared illegal and never implemented. Consequently, the DOH organizational chart was characterized for a long time by ad hoc structures, and staff held contractual rather than permanent *plantilla* (civil service establishment) positions. (9) The situation was similar in Indonesia, where the national civil service administration could take up to five years to approve a new post. (10)

Second, the definition of personnel management processes after decentralization must proceed in parallel with the design of organizational structures. Decisions on how salary scales and position levels are determined and how recruitment, selection, appointment, performance assessment, or staff discipline will be handled are complex, time-consuming, and subject to the influence of a central civil service agency. Clear definition of these management processes is important, since labor conflicts may result if they are left too vague. Furthermore, since decentralized units may have little experience with human resources management and possess few, if any, human resources management systems, the definition of these processes must be accompanied by the design and implementation of appropriate systems and the training of staff in their use.

Third, existing staff members must be reallocated to new organizational structures. Personal preferences, career ambitions, or fear of change can fill the process of staff reallocation with anxiety and discord. If skilled managers are few, the central-level staff may feel particularly uncomfortable in their proposed new roles as experts and technical advisers and oppose any change. In Papua New Guinea, for example, central-level technical officers who were not well qualified for the role of expert adviser at the time of decentralization vigorously resisted revising the organizational structure. (6)

Fourth, the personnel files of decentralized health workers must be transmitted to the management level that is now responsible for them. Compiling an accurate personnel record for each individual, with data on their qualifications and training, employment, salary history, and record of performance, together with physically transferring these records, can be a mammoth task. In Mexico, for example, devolution of health services involved the transfer of 116,000 health workers to the state governments. (11) Transferring the personnel records of this many people creates enormous opportunity for unintended mistakes, which can sour relationships and take considerable time and effort to set straight.

Fifth, mechanisms are required to mediate disputes that may arise between the central and local levels. A chief official at the decentralized management level may, for legitimate reasons of efficiency or resource constraint, refuse to accept a particular post into the organizational structure. Differences in personality or political views between local health staff and local politicians may make the appointment of a particular individual to that geographic area difficult. In the Philippines, local chief executives were unwilling to absorb over 4 percent of DOH personnel by the time the full transfer of assets to local government units (LGUs) was to have been completed. (5) Even if the central level retains the legal power to force the appointment, a health worker's chance of performing his or her duties successfully in such a hostile environment is threatened.

Finally, managers must decide how to deal with health workers who will not or cannot transfer to their new jobs. These health workers may object to physical relocation because of family problems or lack of accommodation in the new locale. Even when workers remain in the same locale, their previous lines of communication and authority are likely to be altered. Since individual health workers develop strong loyalties to their coworkers, the patients they serve, and the location they work in, uprooting, whether it be geographic or emotional, is painful.

Staff transfers are particularly opposed when workers are concerned about their long-term employment security. Recently, some countries have sought to remove health-sector staff from the civil service, thus creating a situation that health staff consider fundamentally threatening to their terms and conditions of service. Evidence is accumulating that these fears may not be groundless. The experiences of Zambia and Sri Lanka indicate that compensation for the loss of civil service benefits and conditions of service must be high if health workers are not to be disadvantaged by this change. (8)

There will always be some health workers who are reluctant or unable to accept their new assignments. Health-sector decision makers must decide the extent to which they are willing to accommodate individual preferences and what sanctions they will apply in the cases of those who refuse to transfer.

Impact of Professional Associations, Unions, and Registration Bodies

Health workers' associations, unions, and registration bodies are a powerful force in the design and implementation of decentralized management structures and jobs. A common fear among health workers is that decentralization will jeopardize their tenure or substantially reduce their salaries and benefits. The issue of labor relations is at the forefront in South Africa, where the disparity between local government staff and employees of provincial health departments (the former can earn 40 to 70 percent more than the latter) is a critical issue facing the Government in its effort to institute a unified, district-based health system that provides care in an equitable manner to all South Africans. (7) Finally, professional registration bodies may be reluctant to approve innovations that successful decentralization demands, such as reallocation of responsibilities between professional cadres, reprofiling of jobs, or changes in the training curriculum and level of entry.

Morale and Motivation of Health Staff

Issues of morale and motivation of health workers loom large during the initial period of decentralization, when new structures, roles, and responsibilities are defined and staff transfers implemented. Uncertainty over their own professional futures and legitimate concern about the impact of decentralization on the quality of health services combine to make this a time of high anxiety for health workers. This anxiety may force some of them to seek employment in the private sector or even outside the country. The loss of morale and motivation can also result in the initial withdrawal of health managers, particularly those at the central level, from planning for decentralization. If these managers fail to engage actively in the early debates over decentralization, they miss an important opportunity to influence the design of new structures and roles.

Collaborative relationships between central and local staff may become frayed when a considerable difference of opinion exists about the advisability of decentralization or the speed with which it is being implemented. Central-level staff may be reluctant to hand power over to local staff, seeing them as ill prepared for their new responsibilities. Local staff, in turn, may be eager to gain a bigger say in the management of health services and resent the slow pace of reforms. Jealousy over perceived individual gains and losses from decentralization may further damage relations between individual staff members.

Decentralization frequently increases local staff's sense of vulnerability to political crossfire. In Papua New Guinea, decentralization provoked not only an intense power struggle between central and provincial health staff but also a continuing conflict in many provinces between provincial politicians and public servants. (12) Few decentralizing health systems have given sufficient attention to developing conflict-resolution mechanisms that provide for timely action in defusing friction.

After the Fact: Decentralized Powers and Human Resources

Decentralization is a complex process, frequently undertaken with some urgency and in a highly political environment. Implementation pressures can force decisions that, in retrospect, are detrimental to guaranteeing equitable, efficient, and competent staffing of health services. This lack of a comprehensive assessment of the human resources implications of decentralization is common. In this section, the key human resources domains where problems arise are identified, and examples of decentralization's impact are provided.

Organizational Structures, Roles, and Responsibilities

Successful decentralization requires that the new organizational structures, roles, and responsibilities be clearly defined, form a functional whole, and be acceptable to the health staff. A review of decentralization in 10 countries demonstrated that this is one of the most problematic areas for human resources. (1) Difficulties arise for several reasons. First, the definition of organizational structures, roles, and responsibilities may be unclear or inappropriate in view of health-sector needs. Second, the roles and responsibilities may conflict with one another. Third, the organizational structures and the allocation of responsibilities may be disputed. Fourth, these organizational changes may be inadequately communicated below the central level or change so frequently that no one is clear on the current status.

The organizational structures, roles, and responsibilities of the intermediate regional level appear to be the hardest to define clearly. The Philippines experience is an interesting case. At the time of devolution, the central DOH retained a regional health office structure consisting of regional field offices whose purpose was to serve as "technical resource management centers directing the flow and utilization of DOH-provided assistance to LGUs." (13) Although this provided a general guideline about their role, translating it into operational detail took several years. Many questions arose. What exactly was the role of the regional level in negotiating Comprehensive Health Care Agreements between the DOH and the LGUs? What was its role in monitoring compliance? How were regional staff expected to support donor-funded projects? Further confusion arose when the DOH established Health, Environment, and Development Zones. These covered wider geographic areas than the regional field offices, and some regional directors were appointed as zone directors. Because other regional directors were not replaced when they resigned, the survival of the regional field offices was quickly perceived to be in doubt.

Defined roles and responsibilities are sometimes in direct conflict with one another. In Papua New Guinea, where the central level retained responsibility for formulating national health policy, each province was responsible for developing its own health policies. (4) The demarcation line between national and provincial policies was not clear, however. For example, given the limited number of trained doctors in the country, the national policy stated that physician resources should be reserved only for staffing hospitals. Some provinces, however, formulated their own human resources policies of staffing key health centers with doctors. They were able to implement this policy by supplementing rural physicians' salaries from provincially raised revenue or by recruiting expatriate volunteers. Inevitably, the equity of medical staffing in the country suffered.

The allocation of roles and responsibilities can be disputed for a number of reasons. Personality conflicts, mistrust, professional pride, or jealousy can all arise in the course of implementing decentralization. A frequent problem involves the relationship between hospital directors and local health managers. Hospital directors in most countries are senior physicians. Considerable resentment may be caused when these doctors are made subordinate to a local health manager who is junior in age and experience. This was the case in Nicaragua, where the conflict resulted in the removal of the five largest hospitals from the control of the local "integrated local health administrative systems" where they were geographically located. (14)

Finally, the organizational structures and roles may be defined and redefined with such frequency that no stakeholder can maintain an accurate comprehension of them. If adequate information about these changes is not transmitted beyond the central level, health workers' adjustment to a new, decentralized health system will not be smooth. In a study by Gilson and colleagues in South Africa, for example, service providers in all provinces indicated that they were only vaguely aware of the content of decentralization policy discussions. Their high level of job insecurity was thought to be generated, at least in part, by the lack of clarity about the way decentralization would change their work and responsibilities. (7)

Viability of Coordinated Health and Human Resources Development

The human resources function must contribute effectively to making strategic choices about the fundamental reforms in financing, organization, and staffing that are essential for developing a nation's health sector. As the 1990 World Health Organization study group on coordinated health and human resources development emphasized, "human resources have no meaning in isolation, but are an instrument for delivering necessary health care." (15) Thus, health services and health personnel planning, production, and management must be well coordinated. There is a real danger, however, that if adequate care is not taken when new organizational structures are designed and powers allocated, decentralization will jeopardize this coordinated development of health services and their staffing.

First, coordinating the development of health services with that of human resources to operate those services requires both reliable data on the numbers, skills, and geographic distribution of health personnel and the capacity to use these data for human resources planning. Decentralization, unfortunately, has the potential to fragment human resources databases by transferring the responsibility for maintaining staff records to decentralized units that lack the necessary systems and skills. This reduces the national capacity for coherent human resources planning. In Papua New Guinea, for example, devolution of power to the provincial level was accompanied by a rapid deterioration of readily usable, reliable information on the number of created positions, vacancies, and training intakes and outputs. (4)

Second, coordinating health and human resources development requires that the allocation of human resources be timely and equitable. If the responsibility for service provision is decentralized to local health managers but the allocation of human resources is left to institutions without technical health knowledge, such as a ministry of civil service, the staffing of health facilities can become inefficient and unbalanced. This was the case in Tanzania and also in Papua New Guinea. In Tanzania, health staff were to be allocated among district health facilities by the District Executive Director (an employee of the Ministry of Local Governments, Cooperatives, and Marketing) on the advice of a district medical officer (DMO). Gilson and colleagues found that in practice, these allocation decisions depended on political and other forces, not only on the advice of the DMO. The result was an unbalanced staffing of facilities, for example, one dispensary with a total of 34 staff members compared with an average of 5 or 6. (16) In Papua New Guinea, where a national Department of Public Services approved the number of health posts, a study of the distribution of rural health workers demonstrated that the allocation of staff to individual rural health facilities was not related to existing workloads. (17)

Third, if decentralization isolates national-level decision making on health and human resources development from local-level staffing decisions, the ensuing conflict and lack of coordination have potentially serious consequences for the equitable, affordable, and competent staffing of health facilities. For example, local aspirations are almost certain to take precedence over the greater national good when a decentralized level is given both considerable freedom to decide how it will develop and staff its health services and the means to generate revenue to pay for such services. The situation is further complicated if the health workers who transfer take their civil service positions with them, as is the case in Nicaragua. (18)

The equity of staff distribution is endangered unless mechanisms exist to expose staffing decisions to national debate and then address the imbalances. Following decentralization in Papua New Guinea, for example, the geographic equity in staff distribution among provinces decreased, as measured by a ratio of health personnel to population. (12) Rural health service staffing suffered because many provinces created a large administrative structure at the provincial health office with staff positions at higher civil service grades than before decentralization. Civil service grades and benefits for positions of equal responsibility and authority were no longer similar among provinces, and in some provinces, the top positions were at even higher civil service grades than comparable national positions.

Fourth, the coordination of health and human resources development can be threatened by decentralization-induced difficulties in career development. Such difficulties can arise either through hindrances to career mobility brought about by decentralization or from a lack of access to continuing education. Particularly in countries where health workers come under local government authority, decentralization can severely restrict access to career opportunities beyond the worker's current administrative area. A transfer to a post in another administrative area may require a resignation from the current post and an accompanying loss of benefits. The transfer from one decentralized unit (such as a province) to another may also require the approval of the administrative head of both the sending and the receiving governmental entity. Understandably, managers are reluctant to lose their most valuable employees and may refuse to approve such a transfer. Even if approval is forthcoming, the bureaucratic delay in arranging the necessary paperwork can be substantial. Such problems may also complicate the management of specialty training programs involving rotating appointments. Finally, staff development opportunities may be restricted because some lower-level units have little or no capacity to mount a program of in-service training for local health staff or because the central level fails to allocate attractive overseas training opportunities equitably.

Finally, staff with special skills, such as health economics or epidemiology, are scarce and are generally best utilized at a central level. Decentralization can complicate their effective functioning by restricting their access to necessary data or by hindering the implementation of their recommendations.

Sustaining an Appropriate Training Capacity

Training institutions should operate within a central framework for the categories and numbers of staff that a nation requires and in accordance with established guidelines and standards on the content and curricula of training. Few decentralizing countries have a clear national human resources plan that is linked to a health systems development plan and is used to guide decisions on the number and types of staff needed. Guidelines and standards for training, in turn, are often unavailable or at least outdated in view of the changes that decentralization has brought about. This is a key concern facing the Zambian government, which intends to make health training institutions semiautonomous under the management of their hospital boards. (19)

Ensuring Technical and Managerial Competence

Ensuring the technical and managerial competence of health workers through the turbulence of decentralization is a major challenge. The transfer of power raises several complex issues that, alone or in combination, jeopardize the competence with which health workers discharge their new duties.

The first issue is a shortage of skilled staff. The new organizational structures and staffing levels may require a quantity of technically trained health staff, especially managers, that the country simply does not possess. In some countries, the shortage is made worse by the reluctance of highly skilled health workers, such as doctors, to move out of the capital city. In countries where expatriate staff are recruited for government positions to compensate for this shortage, these workers face both considerable obstacles to maintaining the technical quality of their work, such as their limited knowledge of local languages and culture, and resentment by some of their national colleagues. (20)

Although the numbers of central- and peripheral-level managers may be sufficient, these managers may not be equipped with the requisite skills for their postdecentralization roles. Bossert points out that central officials must possess skills in policy making and monitoring, whereas lower-level officials need more operational and entrepreneurial skills. (21)

A common finding at the country level is that almost all training efforts concentrate on lower-level staff, and the capacity building of central-level managers is given far too little attention. (1) Management training for local-level health managers, who frequently have little relevant management experience, often consists of a set of uncoordinated, theoretical courses, workshops, and seminars. These training efforts are commonly organized by centrally run vertical programs with donor funding and do not provide practical skills or management tools. Little time is left for the staff to apply what they have learned to their own work settings. (22) An exception to this pattern is the Diploma in Community Medicine program that the Faculty of Medicine at the University of Papua New Guinea set up after decentralization, which was intended to systematically train health workers for senior provincial health management positions. (4)

Peripheral health managers may receive sufficient training in management, but if the control of resources remains centralized and the newly trained managers are not allowed to use their skills, they are likely to become frustrated and leave the service. The resulting turnover of staff reduces the technical competence of the health service, unless sufficient resources are available to quickly train new staff members to replace those who leave.

Shifting roles may impair the quality and frequency of the supervision and support that individual health workers receive. Perhaps the most difficult shift is when the previous supervisory system operated on the basis of professional lines of authority (i.e., doctors supervising doctors and nurses supervising nurses) but local health staff are now expected to operate under a dual supervisory system. Their technical guidance comes from the central health administration, while administrative supervision comes from the local government chief administrator. The line between technical guidance and administrative supervision is not clear, however. Ill-advised administrative decisions may be in conflict with technical guidance and thus seriously harm the quality of the health care provided.

In their study of decentralization from the provincial to the district level in Papua New Guinea, Campos-Outcalt and his colleagues noted that when the district health staff came under the authority of District Assistant Secretaries, any consensus as to who was responsible for monitoring quality was lost. (23) Provincial and district health staff complained about insufficient professional supervision and support and about inappropriate decisions made by the District Assistant Secretaries. They were almost unanimous in their view that the health services were worse off than before decentralization.

Finally, decentralization can politicize decisions on hiring, performance assessment, and staff discipline at the decentralized level so that competence is no longer the basis for hiring and rewards. (4) Although the forces of nepotism and favoritism undoubtedly existed before decentralization, the experience of many countries has been that they become much more difficult to resist when both health managers and politicians live and interact in the same smaller provincial or district headquarters, away from the capital city.

Securing Adequate Performance Conditions

Health workers are not able to deliver high-quality health services on a continuous basis if they are preoccupied with providing for their families' needs or lack the necessary pharmaceuticals, equipment, and transport for their work. Decentralization can have a negative impact on both the timely payment of wages and benefits and the availability of essential resources. The recent experiences of Papua New Guinea and the Philippines illustrate these concerns.

In Papua New Guinea, church health services provide about half of all rural health care, are well integrated with public-sector health services, and receive government subsidies. Recent reforms, which were intended to hand more power to the local government level, failed to clarify the relative responsibilities of provincial and local governments. When several of these governments failed to pay the church health subsidy, the churches suffered a severe funding crisis. The national Department of Health became concerned about the situation but was unable to resolve the crisis promptly, because it involved fundamental decisions about the roles and responsibilities of the national, provincial, and local governments. Church health workers were not paid for several months, and the churches in a number of provinces were forced to close their health services until funds became available. Six months after the first closure of church health services, in July 1997, the outgoing Minister for Provincial and Local Government Affairs (who had previously been the Minister of Health) released the following statement:

> As the outgoing Minister for Provincial and Local Government Affairs, it has been my responsibility to ensure that provinces meet their contractual arrangement with the various churches, including the church health workers who should not be considered as second class citizens, and the churches should not continually be placed in situations where they have to beg for what is rightfully theirs. Either they are paid, or they can take other options to secure the grants, including legal action against the individual provincial governments, and worse still total closure. (24)

In the Philippines, decentralization threatened both the benefits that health workers were entitled to under a central labor agreement (the Magna Carta) and the salary increases that were mandated under the national Salary Standardization Law. The financial base for devolved functions was inadequate, because the variable cost of devolved functions was not congruent with the fixed formula that was used to allocate national revenue among the LGUs. (5) The poorer LGUs were simply unable to fund the payment of Magna Carta benefits and salary increases. LGU executives in the poorer LGUs were probably not very motivated to push for extra funding from their own resources, since the financial compensation of devolved health workers in these LGUs was higher than that of the local mayor.

Without adequate resources, health workers do not have even the minimal performance conditions for competent delivery of health care. A study of health system performance in Papua New Guinea after decentralization showed that budget cuts disproportionately affected funding for transport. This seriously reduced health workers' ability to undertake mobile maternal and child health patrols, disease control activities, and supervisory visits. (25) In the Philippines, a survey of over 5,600 local government officials and health workers assessed the impact of devolution on health services in June 1994. Of the respondents, 46 percent stated that emergency room drugs were never available after devolution, and 61 percent said that operating room drugs were never available. (5) Prior to devolution, these drugs had generally been available.

Recommendations for Health Managers

The previous pages have described several discouraging examples of the impact of decentralization on the availability, competence, and motivation of health workers. Although some of these repercussions may have been foreseen by those designing the decentralization processes or at least feared by the health workers themselves, many were not anticipated. Taken by surprise, health managers were ill prepared to respond promptly to the complex issues that arose and to the multiple institutional actors. This section aims to extract from those examples a few key recommendations to help other health managers who are considering decentralization or already find themselves in its midst.

Become an Advocate for Human Resources

Human resources issues need an advocate in all decentralization debates. Many voices clamor for attention in the fray of decentralization, but regrettably, the cause of human resources development is rarely among them. All health managers should see themselves as champions of the cause of ensuring equitable, competent, and affordable staffing of health services after decentralization.

Anticipate and Prepare for the Cost and Complexity of Decentralization

The complexity of decentralization requires a wide perspective in envisioning the type of human resources issues that are likely to rise. Decentralization carries both financial and emotional costs, and managers must anticipate and be prepared to answer the following kinds of questions:

- How will the future roles of central and local staff be defined?
- How will future planning decisions on the number and type of staff that the nation should develop be made?
- How and by whom will decisions on the staff strength of each decentralized administrative entity be made?
- How will personnel information be gathered and databases maintained?
- How will salaries be set and paid for?
- Is this arrangement financially viable in the long term?
- What will happen to pensions and other benefits?
- Will established career structures be maintained?
- Will in-service and continuing training opportunities at the decentralized level be sufficient to ensure career development?
- How will staff performance be assessed, and by whom?
- Who will be responsible for hiring and firing at the local level?
- What mechanisms will be put in place to address personnel grievances?
- What will be the procedures for transferring health staff from one authority to another?
- What will be the new roles and responsibilities of training institutions?
- What legal implications will decentralization have for the duties and rights of health workers?

By anticipating such questions, health managers can marshal their own resources and, if necessary, call for additional support to respond to these issues in a timely manner.

Develop a Strategic Human Resources Development Capability

Appropriately trained human resources that are equitably distributed and in sufficient quantity are essential for ensuring sustainable benefits from structural and financial reforms in the health sector. A strategic decision-making capability for human resources development at the central and local levels is an essential component of decentralization if human resources planning, training, and management are to support needed health-sector reform measures. The development of such a capacity requires a concerted effort in many areas.

First, a fundamental change is needed in the roles of central- and peripheral-level managers. The human resources unit in most ministries of health confines its activities to personnel administration and training, neglecting strategic thinking about future staffing of health services to meet the requirements of health-sector development. After decentralization, the central human resources unit must focus on formulating strategic options for developing human resources in coordination with health services development, and on monitoring the equity and quality of staffing.

Although the specific role of managers at a decentralized level regarding human resources functions depends on the type and pace of reform and the capacities available at the local level, these peripheral health managers must be represented in all strategic discussions about the future staffing of health services. They also have an important role in developing and implementing performance management mechanisms that improve health workers' productivity and the quality of their work.

Second, readily available, accurate information on human resources, including data on the expenditure on available staff, is essential for strategic development of human resources. If deficiencies are noted in this area, central- and local-level managers must agree on the data that will be collected, how the data are to flow through the health system, who will analyze them, and what the process will be for taking action on the basis of those analyses.

Third, a rational basis must be developed for making human resources decisions, and it must be acceptable to both central and decentralized health authorities. Staffing norms that are based on workloads, such as the Workload Indicators of Staffing Need, are important guides for planning staff requirements and allocating staff to facilities. (26) Guidelines setting out minimum qualifications for a post ensure that staff possess the necessary training. Performance assessment instruments assist managers in making decisions about the level of competence of their staff and what in-service training they need, and procedures for staff discipline foster fair and impartial decision making.

Finally, a strategic view of human resources development under decentralization requires an ongoing assessment of the performance conditions that health workers face in their new roles. If decentralization is found to seriously damage performance conditions, human resources managers must voice their concern and advocate for improvements. This may require working with central financial authorities to secure health workers' salaries and benefits, improving pharmaceutical procurement mechanisms to guarantee availability of essential drugs, or lobbying decentralized government authorities for adequate transport funds for mobile health activities.

Invest in Developing Staff

The change in roles and responsibilities that decentralization generates brings a demand for new skills. Prominent among these are financial, human resources, and logistical management skills, as well as competence in advocacy and negotiation. Investing in staff development at both the central and local levels brings big dividends in determining the eventual success of decentralization. Training must be practical and firmly focused on new job requirements. It must be wide in scope, involving both central and local managers. It must be continual so that the rapid staff turnover that often accompanies decentralization does not dilute the training efforts.

Monitor the Impact of Decentralization on Human Resources Development

Regular monitoring is essential to keep decentralization-related human resources concerns from growing into major problems that take considerable time and resources to solve. Such monitoring should focus on the *equity* of staff distribution, the *access* to skilled care, and the *quality* and *efficiency* of health personnel.

Monitoring should commence with the collection of baseline data before the start of decentralization and continue as an ongoing component of health-sector management. It requires the design and implementation of suitable management processes for ongoing data collection, analysis, and interpretation. Most importantly, it must result in action based on the findings. Such action, in turn, is greatly facilitated if appropriate linkages have been developed between the different institutional actors who influence human resources decisions.

In conclusion, the examples of decentralization's impact on human resources and the lessons derived from them should be seen as an alert about the importance of human resources issues in planning and implementing decentralization. The full implications of decentralization for human resources demand further study and examination. Interested readers may wish to consult three additional documents: a description of one approach to dividing human resources functions between the central and local levels that is included in the WHO human resources toolkit, (27) a decentralization matrix for human resources that the Pan American Health Organization is developing, (28) and the checklists for human resources analysis published by the European Commission. (8)

References

1. Kolehmainen-Aitken, R.-L., and W. Newbrander. *Decentralizing the management of health and family planning programs.* Lessons from FPMD Series. Boston: Management Sciences for Health, 1997.

2. Cassels, A. *Health sector reform: Key issues in less developed countries.* Forum on Health Sector Reform Discussion Paper No. 1. WHO/SHS/NHP/95.4. Geneva: WHO, 1995.
3. WHO Study Group. *The role of research and information systems in decision-making for the development of human resources for health.* Technical Report Series 802. Geneva: WHO, 1990.
4. Kolehmainen-Aitken, R.-L. The impact of decentralization on health workforce development in Papua New Guinea. *Public Administration and Development*, 12:175–91, 1992.
5. Pérez, J., M. C. Alfiler, and M. Victoriano. *Managing transition dilemmas in the early years of devolution in the Philippines.* Decentralization and Health Systems Change Project. Geneva: WHO; Manila: Department of Health, October 1995.
6. Reilly, Q. The transition to decentralization. In: J. Thomason, W. C. Newbrander, and R.-L. Kolehmainen-Aitken, eds. *Decentralization in a developing country: The experience of Papua New Guinea and its health service.* Canberra: Australian National University, National Centre for Development Studies, 1991, pp. 56–57.
7. Gilson, L., R. Morar, Y. Pillay, L. Rispel, V. Shaw, S. Tollman, and C. Woodward. *Decentralization and health system change in South Africa.* Johannesburg: Health Policy Coordinating Unit, March 1996.
8. Martineau, T., and J. Martínez. *Human resources in the health sector: Guidelines for appraisal and strategic development.* Health and Development Series Working Paper No. 1. Brussels: European Commission, January 1997.
9. Kolehmainen-Aitken, R.-L. *Evaluation report: The Philippines Local Government Unit Performance Program (LPP).* Family Planning Management Development. Boston: Management Sciences for Health, September 1995.
10. King, D. Y. Civil service policies in Indonesia: An obstacle to decentralization? *Public Administration and Development* 8:249–60, 1988.
11. De la Fuente, J. R., Secretary for Health, Government of Mexico. Presentation at Harvard University, John F. Kennedy School of Government, September 25, 1997.
12. Thomason, J. A., R.-L. Kolehmainen-Aitken, and W. C. Newbrander. Decentralization of health services in Papua New Guinea: A critical review. In: J. Thomason, W. C. Newbrander, and R.-L. Kolehmainen-Aitken, eds. *Decentralization in a developing country: The experience of Papua New Guinea and its health service.* Canberra: Australian National University, National Centre for Development Studies, 1991.

13. Kolehmainen-Aitken, R.-L. *Assessment of appropriate roles for DOH Regional Field Offices in light of devolution and in support of the LGU performance program in the Philippines.* Family Planning Management Development. Boston: Management Sciences for Health, 1994.
14. Kolehmainen-Aitken, R.-L., M. Mitchell, and W. Newbrander. *Decentralizing health services: What can we learn from country experience?* Presentation at the American Public Health Association 122nd annual meeting, Washington, DC, November 1, 1994.
15. WHO Study Group. *Coordinated health and human resources development.* Technical Report Series 801. Geneva: WHO, 1990.
16. Gilson, L., P. Kilima, and M. Tanner. Local government decentralization and the health sector in Tanzania. *Public Administration and Development* 14:451–77, 1994.
17. Thomason, J. A., and R.-L. Kolehmainen-Aitken. Distribution and performance of rural health workers in Papua New Guinea. *Social Science and Medicine* 32(2):159–65, 1991.
18. Bryant, M., W. Santis, J. Pollock, and J. Eckroad. *Preliminary report on the midterm internal evaluation: Nicaragua Decentralized Health Services Project.* Boston: Management Sciences for Health, July 1997.
19. Huddart, J. Personal communication, June 1997.
20. Gilson, L., and P. Travis. *Health system decentralization in Africa: An overview of experiences in eight countries.* A background document prepared for the regional meeting on Decentralization in the Context of Health Sector Reform in Africa. Geneva: WHO, 1996.
21. Bossert, T. Decentralization. In: K. Janovsky, ed. *Health policy and systems development: An agenda for research.* WHO/SHS/NHP/96.1. Geneva: WHO, 1996.
22. Cohen, S., J. N. Mwanzia, I. O. Omeri, and S. N. Ong'ayo. *Decentralisation and health systems change in Kenya.* Decentralization and Health Systems Change Project. Geneva: WHO, July 1995.
23. Campos-Outcalt, D., K. Kewa, and J. Thomason. Decentralization of health services in Western Highlands province, Papua New Guinea: An attempt to administer health service at the subdistrict level. *Social Science and Medicine* 40(8):1091–98, 1995.
24. Barter, P., Minister for Provincial and Local Government Affairs, Government of Papua New Guinea. Quoted in "Churches yet to get health fund." Port Moresby: *The National* newspaper web page, July 22, 1997.
25. Newbrander, W. C., I. W. Aitken, and R.-L. Kolehmainen-Aitken. Performance of the health system under decentralization. In:

J. Thomason, W. C. Newbrander, and R.-L. Kolehmainen-Aitken, eds. *Decentralization in a developing country: The experience of Papua New Guinea and its health service.* Canberra: Australian National University, National Centre for Development Studies, 1991.

26. Kolehmainen-Aitken, R.-L., and P. Shipp. "Indicators of staffing need": Assessing health staffing and equity in Papua New Guinea. *Health Policy and Planning* 5(2):167–76, 1990.

27. Hall, T. L. *Human resources for health: A toolkit for planning, training and management.* Geneva: WHO, May 1997.

28. Barahona, R., Director for Human Resources, Pan American Health Organization. Personal communication, August 1997.

4
Pharmaceutical Management at the Central and Local Levels

Richard Laing

DECENTRALIZATION MEANS DIFFERENT THINGS to different people. Rondinelli and colleagues have suggested the following classification. (1)

- Delegation (transfer of managerial responsibility for defined functions to organizations outside the government structure)
- Deconcentration (transfer of some authority and responsibility to lower levels within government ministries and agencies)
- Devolution (transfer of power to subnational units of government outside central government control)
- Privatization (transfer of some government functions to voluntary organizations or private enterprise)

In summary, decentralization means the transfer of some authority and responsibility from the central level to the local level. It may occur because of political decisions or due to struggles from the periphery. It may affect all sectors or only the health sector. The decentralization process is often driven by financial constraints.

Pharmaceutical policy and programming cover both public and private (commercial and nongovernmental) sectors and different levels of the health system (hospitals and primary health care units). Pharmaceutical policy frequently intersects with industrial, social, and financial policies. Changes are occurring against the background of epidemiological transition (shift from acute to chronic disease), new diseases (AIDS, resistant tuberculosis), structural adjustment programs (reduced public-sector revenue, staff, controls), global agreements and trade pacts (World Trade Organization, International Conference on Harmonization), and pressures based on external medical knowledge and innovations. See Figure 4.1.

Pharmaceutical policy and programming cover the following areas:

- Selection
- Procurement
- Distribution
- Rational use
- Financing
- Quality assurance (2)

Selection

At the national level, in addition to drug registration, there needs to be an essential drug list (EDL) of safe, efficacious, and cost-effective drugs. (3) This list can be used for public-sector institutions; offered to private and nongovernmental sectors; and used for decisions on customs tariffs, tax incentives to producers and importers, foreign currency allocations, and so forth. Such a list should ideally be adjusted for the different levels of the health system. A generic drug use policy is easy to enforce in the public sector, but difficult in the private sector. The US example of automatic generic drug substitution may be worth emulating.

At the local level, regular selection of an institutional or regional EDL, derived from the national list, is useful for standardizing procurement, distribution, rational use of drugs, and quality assurance. Selection may be made by drug and therapeutic committees in hospitals or by regional or district drug committees. Such selection must involve end users.

Figure 4.1 Selection Issues

- Changing disease spectrum—acute to chronic, new diseases (AIDS, etc.)

- Trade pact pressures

- External medical knowledge pressures

- Innovation pressures—"New is better!"

Procurement

At the national level, government may regulate procurement, undertake tenders in different ways, or shift public-sector procurement to local levels. When governments place tenders and stock large reserves, inefficiencies and wastage occur, even though prices may be good. If procurement is shifted to local levels, efficiency may or may not improve, costs inevitably increase, and opportunities for corruption expand.

The Indonesian and eastern Caribbean systems, in which central tendering for price on an "as needed" basis is combined with distribution by suppliers to local district or country stores, appear to be optimal. Nongovernmental organizations have effectively combined their purchasing power to provide efficient, high-quality, low-cost drugs in a number of African countries. The large nonprofit suppliers, such as the International Dispensary Association (IDA), offer alternatives to centralized procurement.

The private sector also faces choices in procurement between multinational and local suppliers. Particularly when national, private-sector companies combine production, distribution, and retail sale (vertical integration), challenges exist.

Distribution

In this area of pharmaceutical management, the private sector has a clear advantage in transporting drugs from the center to towns and hospitals. Frequently, private-sector distributors are more efficient in managing warehouses or local storage depots. Problems do exist, at least in the public sector, in transferring drugs to the most peripheral health units. Lessons from the private sector may help the public sector deal with this problem, however. Small drugstores abound in remote areas of Nepal and Bangladesh. In these countries, storekeepers fetch their own drugs to ensure that they have something to sell.

Rational Use of Drugs

This is a complex area in which both the central and local levels have a role to play. The central level needs to develop widely accepted standard treatment guidelines (STGs). These should be used for selection of the EDL; procurement and distribution of drugs to different levels of the health system; training and examination of students; and monitoring, audit, and evaluation of performance at facilities. It may be easier for the central government to encourage or enforce the use of STGs in the public sector (central and local). Enforcing their use in the private sector may be impossible. However, decentralized health authorities may find these STGs useful for management and for defining what should be done at which level.

The central government may also have an important role in providing impartial information for prescribers, dispensers, and consumers. This service may be contracted to a drug information center placed in a university or the drug regulatory authority. Privatizing this service may be dangerous.

Financing

When the central government decentralizes services, a major motivation may be to reduce expenditures and increase revenues. Varied experiences exist. Initial efforts to increase fees locally have led to dramatic declines in utilization. More recent studies suggest that if quality improvements occur, utilization may actually increase. The Bamako Initiative was an effort to generate funds locally through drug sales to fund primary health care activities. Major problems exist with this initiative, and few schemes have proved to be successful and sustainable.

When financing systems are restructured, as occurred in Kenya, changes may be neutral or even beneficial for pharmaceutical management. If financing reforms are not clearly thought out, however, negative consequences, such as bypassing of facilities or inappropriate prescribing, may result.

Although central expenditures may decline, there is no guarantee that total expenditures will decrease. Rather, the opposite is likely to occur due to inefficiencies in procurement, losses in local storage and distribution, and polypharmacy. Revenue generation at local levels may also increase, though not enough to match the extra expenditures.

Quality Assurance and Regulation

In this area, the central government must continue to play a major role. Drug registration needs to be centralized and adequately funded. When drug registration is decentralized, as occurred in India, or deregulated, as happened in Peru and Bolivia, major problems occur. Reciprocal recognition of registration has great risks if applied retrospectively. Registration of producers, importers, distributors, and retail outlets is also needed, although enforcement may need to be decentralized.

Quality assurance encompasses more than testing. It relates to all aspects of pharmaceutical system management, which may be deficient in peripheral facilities or areas. The role of quality assurance laboratories is controversial. Few government quality assurance labs function efficiently. This is an area in which contracting with university, private, or international laboratories may be the most sensible option.

Discussion

Although there is a great deal of rhetoric about decentralization improving efficiency, the evidence is mixed. Decentralization is inequitable by its nature, and if pharmaceutical management resources are inequitably distributed, the poor districts or regions will inevitably get worse.

The central government can help the process of decentralization by:

1. Doing what it should do better:
   - EDL selection
   - Development of STGs
   - Regulatory and quality assurance activities
   - Procurement tenders on an "as needed" basis with private-sector distribution

2. *Not* doing what it does poorly:
   - Managing large central stores
   - Distributing drugs
   - Delivering services
   - Directly training or supervising staff

3. Assisting local authorities to be more efficient:
   - Developing simple stock management and financial systems
   - Providing STGs and appropriate training materials
   - Removing tax and tariff obstacles
   - Defining simple quality assurance measures for inspections and drug testing
   - Encouraging local financing systems that do not encourage excessive drug prescribing (such as fee-for-service)
   - Assisting local authorities to procure essential drugs efficiently

4. Educating the public about the new system of pharmaceutical management:
   - Explaining what the central government will continue to do and what will be done locally
   - Providing impartial information on drugs
   - Providing comparative price lists

Decentralization can affect pharmaceutical supply profoundly. Some aspects can be beneficially decentralized, but others should never be decentralized. The process of deciding which functions fall into which camp is complex and difficult. There will be differences among countries and, over time, within countries.

References

1. Rondinelli, D., J. Nellis, and G. Cheema, *Decentralization in developing countries: A review of recent experience.* World Bank Staff Working Paper No. 581, 1984.
2. Management Sciences for Health and the World Health Organization. *Managing drug supply*, 2nd ed. West Hartford, CT: Kumarian Press, 1997.
3. World Health Organization. *The use of essential drugs.* Seventh report of the WHO Expert Committee. WHO Technical Report Series No. 867, 1997.

5
A New Management Information Strategy for Decentralized Public Health Services in the Philippines

Robert J. Timmons, Jose R. Rodriguez, and Florante P. Magboo

NATIONAL GOVERNMENTS HAVE TYPICALLY invested heavily in health management information systems (MIS) that depend on the steady flow of program information from community health centers to national offices. However, the merits of an approach that relies on client records and occasional national surveys to monitor and evaluate family planning and maternal and child health (MCH) programs are questionable. For governments that have transferred the responsibility for planning, organizing, delivering, and financing public health services to the local level, the need for a different approach is evident. With decentralization comes an increased demand for an integrated approach that provides disaggregated data for local monitoring, which requires diverse methods to capture data from clients and at-risk populations locally and nationally. Such an integrated approach to monitoring and evaluation may prove attractive to local and national governments because it focuses on collecting only the data that are essential to their needs.

The Philippines devolved health care to Local Government Units (LGUs) in 1991. At the time, the Department of Health (DOH) relied on the Field Health Services Information System (FHSIS) to collect and consolidate data on clients served by 17 primary health care (PHC) programs. FHSIS had been developed to integrate monitoring of PHC programs and expedite processing of data from health centers to the DOH. Its emphasis on consolidating data from health facilities in communities and municipalities for the national government, and its dependence on computerization to do so, made FHSIS a poor fit for the postdevolution era in which LGUs exercise considerable independence.

Five years later, the DOH, with assistance from the US Agency for International Development (USAID), adopted a new national strategy for monitoring and evaluating family planning and MCH services. In this strategy, the national and local governments play complementary roles in monitoring and evaluating family planning and MCH programs. The strategy exploits a variety of data sources at different levels of the health care system to provide appropriate data on client and at-risk populations. It emphasizes the use of community- and facility-based data for decision making at local levels, provincial multi-indicator cluster surveys conducted by local research institutions to measure program performance from public and private sectors, and riders to national annual surveys that serve the interests of many ministries.

Background to the New Strategy

Fertility, mortality, and natural increase in population have declined in the Philippines since the inception of its population program in 1969. The total fertility rate has declined from 5.8 children in 1970 to an estimated 4.1 in 1997. Life expectancy has risen from 55.7 to an estimated 66 years over the same period. Infant mortality has dropped from 56.9 per 1,000 births in 1980 to 34 in 1997. Maternal mortality is 280 per 100,000. The rate of natural increase in population has dropped from 3 percent to 2.3 percent. (1)

According to the 1993 National Demographic Survey, 62 percent of births in the Philippines are high risk. Contraceptive use has doubled from 20 to 40 percent since 1970, and the use of modern methods rose from 15.5 percent in 1980 to 24.9 percent in 1990 to 30.2 percent in 1996. (2) However, there is a substantial unmet need. Fifty-one percent of married women of reproductive age want no

Table 5.1 Devolution in the Philippines

Level	Health Care Responsibilities
DOH	Foreign-funded national programs; experimental national programs; regulation, licensing, and accreditation; regional hospitals; specialized health facilities
LGUs	
Provinces and chartered cities (78)	Hospitals; tertiary services
Municipalities (1,543)	PHC and MCH; disease control; access to secondary and tertiary care; purchase of medicines, supplies, equipment
Barangays (41,924)	Health stations

more children, and 19 percent want to wait two years before having a child. To meet these needs and continue to reduce the total fertility rate to projected levels, the number of married women of reproductive age using contraception must rise from less than 6 million in 1995 to nearly 16 million in 2020.

Starting in 1991, the DOH turned over 595 hospitals; 12,859 rural health units, municipal health centers, and *barangay* (community) health stations; and 46,080 personnel to 78 provinces, 1,543 municipalities, and 41,924 *barangays* (see Table 5.1). As a result, *barangays* became responsible for maintaining health stations, and municipalities became responsible for implementing PHC, MCH, and communicable and noncommunicable disease control services; access to secondary and tertiary health services; and purchase of medicines, supplies, and equipment. Provinces and chartered cities took charge of hospitals and other tertiary health services. The DOH retained components of national programs that are funded from foreign sources; nationally funded programs that are in the process of being pilot tested or developed; health services and disease control programs that are covered by international agreements; regulatory, licensing, and accreditation functions; and regional hospitals, medical centers, and specialized health facilities. (3)

Devolution of health care to LGUs has significantly reduced the reliability of FHSIS data. FHSIS is the DOH's principal monitoring system for 12 programs, but it has struggled for adequate resources. USAID has supported FHSIS's development and cluster surveys in the provinces, and it currently funds an annual national family planning survey and a national demographic survey every five years. The DOH's family planning and MCH services have relied heavily on information from the FHSIS and on occasional national and provincial surveys over the past 10 years. The managers of family planning services have gone directly to the regions for FHSIS data when data were unavailable nationally, but the DOH's MCH services have not received data regularly from FHSIS since devolution. FHSIS reporting to LGUs and the DOH has recently been simplified and pilot tested, and a modified version is being implemented nationwide.

Some national and local nongovernmental organizations (NGOs) are forwarding their service statistics to the public sector to be included in national figures. This practice has led to double counting in some instances. The Social Marketing of Contraceptives Project and major pharmaceutical suppliers use dealer polls and sales reports and conduct drugstore audits four to six times each year to estimate couple-years of protection and contraceptive use.

Strategic Framework

In the future, family planning and MCH services will require that the DOH and LGUs coordinate information activities and share in their funding. LGUs should assume considerable responsibility for monitoring and evaluating the services they deliver as the DOH adapts to its new role of setting the national agenda and providing technical assistance to LGUs.

A monitoring strategy that exploits a variety of data sources at different levels of the health care system is the best choice for decentralized services. The monitoring strategy that Management Sciences for Health has designed asks both the DOH and local governments

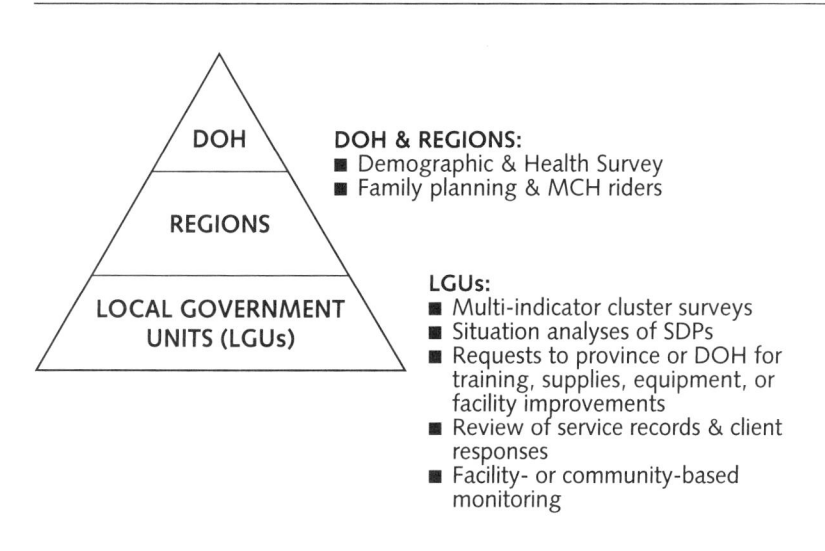

Figure 5.1 MIS Strategy for Family Planning, MCH, and Nutrition Services

```
        /\
       /DOH\           DOH & REGIONS:
      /─────\           ■ Demographic & Health Survey
     /REGIONS\          ■ Family planning & MCH riders
    /─────────\
   /           \       LGUs:
  / LOCAL GOVT. \      ■ Multi-indicator cluster surveys
 /  UNITS (LGUs) \     ■ Situation analyses of SDPs
/─────────────────\    ■ Requests to province or DOH for
                         training, supplies, equipment, or
                         facility improvements
                       ■ Review of service records & client
                         responses
                       ■ Facility- or community-based
                         monitoring
```

to play important roles in monitoring and evaluating the family planning and MCH programs. The strategy emphasizes the use of program data for decision making at local levels; provincial cluster surveys to measure the performance of family planning and MCH programs in the public, nongovernmental, and commercial sectors; and riders to the National Statistics Office's Labor Force Survey and to periodic Demographic and Health Surveys to evaluate impact on the population. Figure 5.1 summarizes this strategy. It shows what sources of data can be used to evaluate quality of care at facilities, utilization of resources, program performance, and population outcomes.

The strategy addresses the key needs identified in two recent studies. A 1996 survey of cooperating agencies conducted for USAID's Center for Population, Health, and Nutrition concluded that information is needed for policy change and reform, program planning, management, resource allocation, and program sustainability. (4) Meeting the needs of host countries and local program managers was viewed as primary. The survey also pointed to a growing need for disaggregated information at local levels for management and planning. The agencies surveyed also concluded that attention needed to be paid to assessing the cost-effectiveness of routine information systems versus surveys.

A recent report took the Philippines as the subject of one of its case studies. The report found that "performance monitoring systems should emphasize the routine examination of data at the level at which they are collected. Even lowly [*sic*] skilled workers can be trained to perform simple monthly or quarterly comparisons. It is evident there is a need to encourage more widespread use of simple, systematic analyses for local program monitoring." (5)

National Information Needs

Among its postdevolution functions, the DOH defines national health policy; formulates and implements the national health plan; and assists, coordinates, or collaborates with local communities, agencies, and international organizations in health-related activities. It also functions to collect, analyze, and disseminate information on the country's health situation; propagate health information and educate the population; undertake health and medical research; and conduct training in support of its priorities, programs, and activities. To discharge these duties, the DOH must know the outcomes from services delivered by LGUs, and it must integrate this information into its strategic planning for the nation.

The DOH needs data on the national health situation as measured by program effects (change in contraceptive prevalence, for example) and impact (change in fertility, for example). However, service providers' unremunerated burden of collecting volumes of data is well known in the Philippines and in many other countries that are developing health MIS. It also comes as no surprise that national health policy makers and program managers have greater confidence in the accuracy of information from surveys and special studies than in information from national service statistics. Findings from recent surveys and from the commodities distribution and logistics MIS verified significant irregularities in national family planning service statistics.

Sources of Information for the National Level

The National Statistics Office, in collaboration with the Health Intelligence Service of the DOH, has conducted the National Health Survey every five years. The most recent one was in 1992. The National Statistics Office has also conducted the National Demographic Survey (one of the demographic and health surveys funded worldwide by USAID) every five years in collaboration with Macro International. The last National Demographic Survey in the Philippines was in 1993. To reduce costs and improve quality, the strategy calls for the DOH to incorporate important health indicators from its National Health Survey into the National Demographic Survey to create one demographic and health survey. A National Demographic and Health Survey was conducted in 1998 by the National Statistics Office with technical assistance from Macro International. The National Statistics Office is also authorized to conduct a census every decade, and sometimes every five years, as was the case in 1990 and 1995. Projections to three years are made based on the censuses for the nation, provinces, and urban and rural areas. The Office plans to update its expanded sample of households annually.

At the national and regional levels, the new strategy will rely heavily on national household surveys. To carry out these surveys cost-effectively, the National Statistics Office, in collaboration with the DOH, is conducting family planning and MCH surveys as riders to its Labor Force Survey each year (except for the years when a National Demographic and Health Survey is conducted). USAID is currently funding the riders. The family planning survey is in its third year, and the first MCH survey was conducted in 1997. Results from past family planning surveys showed an increase in modern contraceptive use and a decrease in traditional method use. Regional contraceptive prevalence varied from 13 percent in the Autonomous Region of Muslim Mindanao (ARMM) to 59.9 percent in Region

XI. Results from the 1997 MCH survey revealed that 58.2 percent of children 12 to 23 months of age were fully immunized by their first birthday, and 52.4 percent of the youngest children were protected against neonatal tetanus. Consolidated service records approximated significantly higher immunization and tetanus coverage in the past. In the future, the DOH will take responsibility for analyzing data from these surveys to facilitate program planning and implementation.

In addition to the national survey riders, use of reversible contraceptive methods is reported by a commodities distribution and logistics MIS supported by USAID. Couple-years of protection, as reported by the commodities distribution and logistics MIS in 1995, represented 19.6 percent (of married women of reproductive age who obtained a reversible method of contraception), compared with the 16.9 percent estimated by the National Statistics Office's family planning survey. Couple-years of protection as reported by the commodities distribution and logistics MIS has been a reasonably reliable proxy of reversible contraceptive use. However, data from the FHSIS showed a much higher percentage (26.8) of married women of reproductive age obtaining a reversible method, excluding the commercial sector. In 1993, FHSIS data showed about 91 percent of children under 12 months of age fully immunized, whereas the National Demographic Survey showed that 71.5 percent of children aged 12 to 23 months were fully immunized. MCH cluster surveys have supported the National Demographic Survey finding. The new strategy expects FHSIS to play a more important role in local decision making for family planning and MCH services rather than in reporting at the national level.

Information Needs of Local Government Units

Sources of Information for Local Government Units

Local governments need information on the effects services have on communities (contraceptive prevalence or proportion of children fully immunized, for example) so that they can better meet people's needs. They also need information on how services are utilized (number of family planning acceptors or number of children vaccinated for measles, for example) to better manage service delivery. Routine health service data are relatively cheap and easy to collect. However, providers are often overburdened by demands to collect data. They are rarely expected to analyze the data themselves, but they do not usually receive feedback from higher levels of authority either. The quality of the data collected, therefore, is often poor, and collecting data is not cost-effective.

Health service statistics can provide information on the number of clients seen or the number of visits, but they rarely provide information on the population at risk or the population covered by the service. Surveys do provide information on program coverage and can complement routine statistics when conducted periodically. In the Philippines, LGUs that allocate program resources to conduct routine cluster surveys for monitoring family planning and MCH services can help fill the gaps in the national health MIS. They can provide a clear picture of target populations at a specific time and, if conducted as planned, can profile the women and children most at risk. Provincial and city officials can use such information to design better family planning and MCH programs and reallocate resources.

LGUs also need to monitor the quality of care delivered at their health facilities. Health facility assessments (situation analyses) have proved to be a quick and effective way to evaluate important elements of service delivery (facility conditions, supplies and equipment, trained personnel, services provided, health worker practices, record keeping, and reporting, for example). It is also reliable and inexpensive to use selected indicators of quality of care from health facility assessments to certify facilities as meeting national standards.

CLUSTER SURVEYS FOR PROVINCES AND CITIES. Specifically, provinces and large cities can complement FHSIS data gathering by conducting multi-indicator cluster surveys annually or as needed based on anticipated achievements (change in an indicator may not be significantly different from the survey's margin of error, thereby necessitating less frequent survey intervals). The DOH, in its new role in the postdevolution era, can assist provinces and cities in planning and budgeting for cluster surveys, and local academic institutions can design, conduct, and report results to governors and mayors and, in turn, to the DOH. Involvement of research institutions geographically distributed throughout the country will also build capacity for local health program planning and implementation and increase the long-term sustainability of monitoring efforts among LGUs. LGUs would be expected to conduct multi-indicator cluster surveys about every three years, and they are encouraged to revise the survey questionnaires to meet their particular information needs, as long as data are collected on a core set of indicators.

SURVEY DESIGN. The DOH chose to use the standard multi-indicator cluster survey (MICS) design documented by UNICEF. (6) The surveys focus on four indicators: contraceptive prevalence (percentage of women of reproductive age who are currently using program or nonprogram family planning methods), the fully immunized child (percentage of living children between 12 and 23 months of age who have been vaccinated before their first birthday against tuberculosis, diphtheria-pertussis-tetanus, polio, and measles), tetanus toxoid coverage (percentage of pregnant women and mothers of reproductive age with children under five who have received at least two doses of tetanus toxoid), and vitamin A coverage among children under five.

Based on the lowest prevalence (coverage) among these indicators and other design considerations, the first round of MICS has each province or city sampling 15 respondents in each of 62 *barangays* (clusters). The number of clusters was increased more than the number of respondents per cluster because *barangays* are considered quite homogeneous, and most of the variability will be explained between *barangays* rather than within them. (7)

This design is used because it is relatively easy to plan and conduct and does not require the listing of households. However, the second stage of sampling uses the random walk method for selecting households, and for this reason, the design does not result in a probability sample (a quota sampling procedure is used such that contiguous households are visited in each cluster until information has been gathered on the required number of the target sample, usually children between 12 and 23 months of age). Therefore, once the random walk method is introduced, the actual margin of error is no longer known. Training of interviewers, ensuring that procedures are followed, and supervision during the survey are critical to accurate statistics.

In subsequent rounds of MICS, provinces and cities may be advised to consider a second-stage method that results in a probability sample at little additional effort and cost. Researchers sketch maps of sample clusters, from which subclusters or segments of about equal size can be created. Then one segment in each cluster is chosen at random, and all individuals in the target groups in all the households in the selected segments are interviewed. Since all households in the segment are chosen, listing of households is not required. (8) Segmenting *barangays* may be difficult, however, because of the considerable variability among urban and rural *barangay* populations.

IMPLEMENTATION. The DOH and many LGUs have experience in planning and conducting cluster surveys. Most LGUs conducted Expanded Programme on Immunization (EPI) cluster surveys between 1990 and 1992. In 1991, the DOH carried out contraceptive prevalence cluster surveys in six selected provinces, and it conducted another 30 in 1993. In 1994, a national, integrated MCH cluster survey was conducted to estimate immunization coverage, use of oral rehydration therapy, management of acute respiratory infection, maternal care and breast-feeding, iron supplementation, and contraceptive prevalence. In 1995, a few more LGUs conducted contraceptive prevalence surveys. Finally, the National Statistics Office, supported by UNICEF, recently conducted a national multi-indicator cluster survey to measure progress toward mid-decade goals for immunization coverage, vitamin A supplementation and dietary education, salt iodization, use of oral rehydration therapy, and water supply and sanitation. For most of these surveys, the DOH provided technical assistance and support. For the 1993 contraceptive prevalence surveys, LGU staff conducted the cluster surveys in other LGUs. International assistance and research institutions have played various roles in planning and conducting the surveys.

As part of the new management information strategy, the DOH, with USAID assistance, asked the 46 LGUs participating in the

LGU Performance Program to complete a questionnaire on their experience with cluster surveys. Of the 27 LGUs that reported, 21 have conducted cluster surveys: 13 have conducted EPI cluster surveys, 5 have conducted contraceptive prevalence cluster surveys, and 3 have carried out multi-indicator MCH cluster surveys. Most of the 27 participated in data collection. Six or 7 participated in data processing and analysis. Ten reported having difficulty locating households and conducting interviews, 4 reported difficulty in processing and analyzing the data, and 5 said that securing funding was difficult.

Most LGUs (18 of 27) want to share responsibility for conducting cluster surveys with research institutions. Nearly all LGUs responded that they can play a major role in training interviewers and in collecting data but need assistance in planning and designing the surveys and analyzing the data. The DOH has identified the research institutions that are most capable of planning and conducting multi-indicator cluster surveys, and the 46 provinces and cities have paired with research institutions mostly within their borders or in their regions. Some of these institutions are experienced in conducting surveys and in working with LGUs. In this first round of MICS, about 30 research institutions were selected to conduct the 47 provincial and city surveys. The DOH can establish a means of accreditation to reduce the field of research institutions to a more manageable size, and provinces and cities may wish to consider competitive bidding among research institutions to control costs.

Results from the 46 LGUs unmask variability that national household surveys hide. For example, Table 5.2 shows that the contraceptive method mix in the LGUs is significantly different but that there are some consistencies within regions. Pills are the most popular modern method in the Philippines, and in Region VI, the modern method used is predominantly pills. However, pill use varies from 11.4 percent in Benguet Province in Cordillera Autonomous Region (CAR), where female sterilization and condom use are high, to 46 percent in Bacolod City in Region VI, where use of all other modern methods is low.

IUD use varies from less than 1 percent to 30.5 percent among LGUs. In Region VI, IUD use is consistently low, but it is consistently high in Region X. Use of injectables varies from a low of 0.4 percent to a high of 15.4 percent. Female sterilization varies from less than 1 percent in Isabela to over 28 percent in Pampanga. However, female sterilization is high in all five LGUs in Region III and in CAR, where it is 24.3 and 24.6 percent in Baguio City and Benguet Province, respectively. In Regions VI and X, female sterilization is consistently low.

Condom use ranges from 0.1 percent in Ilocos Sur Province to 11.2 percent in Benguet Province. Use of the lactational amenorrhea method is greater than 10 percent in five LGUs in four regions. In regions where calendar/rhythm use is high, withdrawal use is low, and vice versa. Among women of reproductive age who are not using any method, 16.2 percent are afraid of side effects.

The MICS also reveal that protection at birth against neonatal tetanus ranges from 37.7 percent in Maguindanao to 86.4 percent in Benguet Province, and 37.3 percent of women not receiving a tetanus toxoid vaccine are not aware of it. Fully immunized child coverage varies from a low of 58.6 percent in Pampanga in Region III to a high of 93.6 in Davao City, Region XI. Zamboanga City in Region IX also has a low coverage rate, whereas the four provinces in Region XI have high coverage rates (see Table 5.3). To estimate fully immunized child coverage, children 12 to 59 months of age rather than children 12 to 23 months were sampled to reduce survey costs for LGUs. Vitamin A coverage during the Knock Out Polio campaign in April 1997 was consistently high. Mothers' not taking their children to the health center is the most important reason for children not receiving vitamin A supplementation (46.7 percent).

Donors with projects in LGUs participating in the LGU Performance Program have shown interest in taking part in and supporting planning and implementation of the proposed multi-indicator surveys. Other USAID institutional contractors have expressed interest in using the MICS to collect data that are important to their project interests.

Table 5.2 Contraceptive Method Use, 1997 Multi-Indicator Cluster Surveys (Percentage)

Region/LGUs	Pill	IUD	Injectable	Female Sterilization	Condom	LAM	Calendar/Rhythm	Withdrawal	Others
Region I									
La Union	38.8	3.4	13.5	11.0	2.8	5.7	17.9	3.0	3.9
Ilocos Sur	34.1	1.8	9.0	10.4	0.1	13.7	11.6	18.6	0.7
Pangasinan	31.7	3.9	13.3	11.3	3.9	2.7	5.7	8.6	18.9
Region II									
Isabela	45.8	11.3	14.2	0.8	1.4	4.5	8.0	4.6	9.4
Cagayan Province	39.8	14.1	7.2	5.8	1.5	12.2	7.0	9.2	3.2
Region III									
Bataan	21.6	6.7	8.2	23.5	2.1	2.4	11.3	23.5	0.7
Bulacan	36.4	3.7	8.4	11.2	5.0	4.2	8.4	20.6	2.1
Tarlac	24.1	7.2	6.8	24.1	1.8	2.5	7.6	24.7	1.2
Pampanga	19.8	0.2	5.9	28.4	2.6	4.2	6.8	31.0	1.0
Nueva Ecija	30.3	5.5	13.5	19.0	0.8	5.5	3.0	21.9	0.5
Region IV									
Cavite	28.3	5.5	9.8	13.3	1.2	9.4	14.6	16.3	1.6
Palawan	39.4	1.6	5.5	10.0	4.3	—	14.1	5.7	19.4
Region V									
Albay	28.9	4.9	9.7	3.5	6.0	3.5	15.1	14.2	14.2
Masbate	56.1	1.6	0.4	5.7	3.3	3.3	15.5	7.9	6.2
Region VI									
Capiz	45.1	6.6	2.9	3.6	0.7	10.3	16.7	12.6	1.5
Iloilo Province	22.6	2.8	9.4	6.9	3.2	9.2	36.1	9.2	0.6
Negros Occidental	37.6	8.6	13.4	2.5	4.7	8.6	17.9	6.5	0.2
Iloilo City	34.9	2.9	3.4	7.4	3.5	13.7	20.4	—	13.8
Bacolod City	46.0	3.6	3.8	4.2	6.6	8.5	20.6	5.3	1.4
Region VII									
Negros Oriental	29.1	19.0	8.1	3.5	3.9	0.2	32.9	5.2	0.4
Bohol	21.2	9.2	10.8	8.5	8.2	1.9	34.6	4.4	1.2
Cebu City	14.9	12.3	12.6	5.6	8.8	9.1	26.6	7.9	2.2
Cebu Province	19.8	12.4	10.4	7.5	6.6	0.4	29.6	12.2	1.1

Region VIII									
Leyte	27.7	8.9	14.0	2.3	2.3	0.6	30.4	13.0	0.8
Region IX									
Zamboanga City	42.9	7.8	9.1	8.9	.4	1.5	20.8	7.1	2.5
Zamboanga del Sur	31.7	16.3	6.2	2.2	1.3	.2	33.3	5.7	3.1
Region X									
Bukidnon	28.3	22.2	11.2	3.1	3.0	0.6	27.5	5.5	—
Cagayan de Oro City	19.4	29.9	11.0	6.5	2.9	0.2	21.2	7.4	1.5
Misamis Oriental	25.1	30.5	9.8	2.2	2.6	0.2	23.7	4.2	1.7
Misamis Occidental	29.8	13.2	9.1	6.9	0.4	0.4	30.7	6.5	3.0
Region XI									
Davao del Sur	28.0	16.5	14.3	2.4	4.2	4.4	21.6	8.1	0.5
Davao City	23.8	17.9	7.7	16.3	2.8	2.8	23.7	3.4	1.6
Davao Norte	29.8	15.5	7.4	12.8	1.7	7.0	21.0	2.3	2.5
South Cotabato	31.8	14.0	12.2	11.5	3.6	1.3	21.9	1.6	2.1
Davao Oriental	24.7	15.4	6.3	12.8	2.1	4.8	30.2	2.3	1.4
Region XII									
North Cotabato	31.4	18.0	14.1	4.3	1.4	10.1	16.7	1.9	2.1
ARMM									
Maguindanao	33.0	14.0	12.0	13.0	4.0	—	20.0	—	4.0
Caraga									
Surigao del Sur	24.5	17.6	13.6	3.2	2.8	6.9	25.1	5.4	0.9
Surigao del Norte	36.8	8.6	15.2	8.9	3.6	2.4	22.3	3.1	—
CAR									
Baguio City	16.9	3.3	15.4	24.3	7.8	2.4	16.0	12.1	1.8
Benguet Province	11.4	3.6	8.7	24.6	11.2	—	17.5	20.1	2.9
NCR*									
Pasig	32.6	3.7	4.5	12.3	5.6	—	13.4	27.6	0.3
Quezon City	27.1	1.9	4.6	13.7	4.4	5.1	17.8	23.2	2.2
Malabon	32.2	8.9	8.0	17.8	2.9	1.7	7.6	19.2	1.7
Muntinlupa	36.1	16.5	3.8	12.0	3.1	2.1	12.4	12.9	1.1
Pasay City	37.4	11.3	2.4	10.6	8.1	1.9	12.4	15.8	0.1

*NCR=National Capital Region

Table 5.3 Fully Immunized Children 12 to 59 Months of Age, 1997 Multi-Indicator Cluster Surveys (Percentage)

Region/LGUs	BCG	OPV3	DPT3	Measles	FIC
Region I					
La Union	—	—	—	—	62.1
Ilocos Sur	97.2	88.8	85.5	84.4	76.9
Pangasinan	89.0	79.3	78.9	75.4	67.1
Region II					
Isabela	69.5	67.6	68.6	66.7	73.5
Cagayan Province	94.3	84.6	84.4	82.9	80.7
Region III					
Bataan	98.5	94.7	94.0	93.1	82.2
Bulacan	93.5	91.8	92.1	90.4	81.7
Tarlac	86.0	75.5	75.6	74.6	73.8
Pampanga	70.9	59.1	59.1	58.6	58.6
Nueva Ecija	70.1	63.3	63.8	63.6	63.3
Region IV					
Cavite	96.6	91.0	92.0	91.4	78.7
Palawan	—	—	—	—	64.8
Region V					
Albay	92.8	87.2	88.8	85.8	80.4
Masbate	78.1	75.0	74.9	75.6	62.8
Region VI					
Capiz	97.1	93.9	93.6	90.1	81.1
Iloilo Province	97.8	96.0	95.8	93.0	88.1
Negros Occidental	99.1	92.9	92.4	92.4	87.2
Iloilo City	93.2	92.9	90.3	96.7	85.0
Bacolod City	99.0	89.3	89.2	88.5	74.6
Region VII					
Negros Oriental	95.4	87.3	87.2	83.9	72.7
Bohol	93.5	87.7	88.2	85.0	79.5
Cebu City	98.7	91.9	91.7	90.3	80.5
Cebu Province	89.6	85.6	85.4	78.3	77.7

Region VIII					
Leyte	99.6	94.7	94.5	91.9	80.5
Region IX					
Zamboanga City	97.3	91.2	90.8	86.5	77.7
Zamboanga del Sur	90.2	87.9	86.1	82.2	81.0
Region X					
Bukidnon	97.1	93.4	92.9	93.2	87.8
Cagayan de Oro City	96.8	93.1	93.2	90.1	89.2
Misamis Oriental	89.2	90.2	90.3	87.2	82.9
Misamis Occidental	84.6	82.9	82.4	80.1	86.7
Region XI					
Davao del Sur	97.3	91.7	90.3	88.8	84.5
Davao City	98.0	97.2	96.6	95.0	93.6
Davao Norte	97.3	96.1	96.2	94.6	93.3
South Cotabato	96.4	95.3	93.9	92.0	88.8
Davao Oriental	99.3	95.8	96.9	95.0	88.0
Region XII					
North Cotabato	96.0	89.0	88.0	86.0	80.0
ARMM					
Maguindanao	81.2	71.0	72.0	74.7	60.2
Caraga					
Surigao del Sur	95.6	90.3	88.7	85.8	80.0
Surigao del Norte	96.9	92.6	92.6	86.8	86.6
CAR					
Baguio City	92.7	89.7	90.0	89.0	81.8
Benguet Province	97.5	93.1	93.3	90.8	73.5
NCR*					
Pasig	96.0	84.4	84.6	80.2	77.4
Quezon City	94.5	88.0	89.2	86.0	80.9
Malabon	99.0	96.0	96.0	94.0	89.0
Muntinlupa	99.0	88.0	89.0	89.0	82.0
Pasay City	98.0	92.0	93.0	92.0	87.0

Sources: Based on vaccination card and verification of mother's recall from health center records.
*NCR=National Capital Region

Health Facility Assessments

Governments often fail to include routine monitoring of their health facilities' preparedness to deliver high-quality services. Information on health program inputs and processes can help managers make well-informed decisions about allocating limited resources or changing delivery procedures. For example, a recorded stockout of pills in a *barangay* or municipality might explain why the number of women who were resupplied with pills decreased in the past quarter. Lack or poor quality of training in certain contraceptive methods might explain why clients are choosing one method disproportionately over all others.

The new strategy will use health facility assessments to periodically evaluate city health centers, municipal and rural health units, and *barangay* health stations in the Philippines. The assessment instruments have been developed as modules for ease of use. A key set of interview questions and observations will be identified to certify that health facilities are meeting standards established by the DOH or are deficient and in need of technical assistance, training, supplies, or equipment. The DOH is initiating facility assessments as part of an annual certification program. Certification teams will be composed of DOH and LGU staff that will target health centers in cities and rural health units in municipalities the first year. Summary reports will be forwarded to the City or Municipal Health Officer and to the Mayor's office. Subsequently, city or municipal staff primarily from health centers or rural health units will be expected to assess and certify *barangay* health stations within their jurisdictions.

In the recent past, provinces and cities participating in the LGU Performance Program were required to complete annual comprehensive plans based on similar information from lower devolved units (*barangay* health stations, rural health units, municipal hospitals, and so forth) and other organizations directly involved in providing services to the target populations. As an annual exercise for provincial and city health or population offices, it has proved to be a difficult process that takes months and produces questionable results.

For this reason, the process has been further decentralized, and the purpose has been changed from preparing a planning document to assessing quality of care at facilities, facility certification, and requests for assistance where deficiencies are found.

Monitoring at Facilities and in Communities

Family planning and MCH clients are served by facility-based staff and by volunteers in *barangays* throughout the nation. Some combination of government community health workers and other volunteers from nongovernmental organizations interacts with midwives at *barangay* health stations to provide services. Some provinces and cities have formed population offices to administer family planning services separately from their health offices. Devolution and the variety of service delivery models for family planning have made it difficult for LGUs to conform to nationally standardized recording and reporting at facilities. Also, low contraceptive prevalence, high unmet need, and the high proportion of married women of reproductive age with pregnancy-related health conditions have led LGU health officials to reinvest in community health worker networks. (9)

FHSIS, the national health information system that consolidates service records at each level of authority, has been difficult to maintain since its inception and was severely hampered by devolution. It is unlikely that FHSIS, even in a modified state, can meet information demands at the local and national levels. Nor should it be expected to. However, community volunteers and staff at health facilities, municipalities, and LGUs need to take advantage of the information available from the delivery of health services. A modified FHSIS that focuses on local levels can provide information on service utilization to help staff make decisions about delivery of services. If emphasis is on the local use of data and not on consolidating and reporting to regional offices and the DOH, LGUs will have some freedom to adapt systems to meet their particular needs.

Recently, the FHSIS has been modified and implemented nationwide. The modified FHSIS produces a "minimum set of indicators" and simplifies the "flow of municipal/city health data to the national level by reducing data volume . . . ; replacing health facility reporting by a municipal/city consolidated reporting; reducing the frequency of the reporting . . . ; and designing both manual and computerized data processing at the provincial level." (10) FHSIS can become an important element of the strategy, especially if it is modified to allow for community-based data gathering and is redirected toward using service statistics locally to manage services.

Conclusions

Although the management information strategy promotes use of different, independent sources of data from a variety of funding sources, sustainability is likely to be a serious concern. Cluster surveys conducted by LGUs participating in the LGU Performance Program will be funded by the project. The family planning and MCH riders to the Labor Force Survey are currently funded by USAID. However, the Family Planning Service of the DOH has increased its annual budget so that it can support the national family planning survey in the future. The strategy's focus on using health facility assessments to monitor quality of care, health service statistics for local decision making, capacity building of regional research institutions to help LGUs conduct cluster surveys, and riders to the National Statistics Office's annual Labor Force Survey are elements of a framework intended to produce comprehensive, high-quality information at a reasonable cost. However, unlike an information system that concentrates on consolidation of health services statistics at all levels and for which costs are rarely disaggregated from other costs, the cost of surveys is usually conspicuous, and surveys are perceived as expensive. LGUs and the family planning and MCH services of the DOH should be vigilant about evaluating the costs and benefits of the information expected to be available if the strategy is enacted and should modify the data collected and the methodologies used as needed.

References

1. *1997 world population data sheet.* Washington, DC: Population Reference Bureau, May 1997.
2. *1996 national family planning survey.* Manila: National Statistics Office, 1996.
3. Pérez, J., M. C. Alfiler, and M. Victoriano. *Managing transition dilemmas in the early years of devolution in the Philippines.* Decentralization and Health Systems Change Project. Geneva: WHO; Manila: Department of Health, October 1995.
4. Foltz, A.-M., and J. Seltzer. *Future priorities for USAID in data collection, monitoring, and evaluation: A survey of population, health, and nutrition cooperating agencies.* Background paper. Washington, DC: USAID, March 1996.
5. *Performance monitoring for family planning and reproductive health programs: An approach paper.* POLICY Project. Glastonbury, CT: The Futures Group, April 20, 1996.
6. *Monitoring progress toward the goals of the World Summit for Children: A practical handbook for multiple-indicator surveys.* New York: UNICEF, January 1995.
7. Expected proportion, 50 percent; estimated number of responses per cluster, 15; rate of homogeneity, 10 percent; confidence level, 95 percent; confidence interval, 5 percent; design effect, 2.4; clusters needed, 62; total responses, 930.
8. Turner, A. G., R. J. Magnani, and M. Shuaib. A not quite as quick but much cleaner alternative to the Expanded Programme on Immunization (EPI) cluster survey design. *International Journal of Epidemiology* 25(1):198–203, 1996.
9. Some LGUs are reinvesting in Barangay Service Point Officers (BSPOs) and are interested in rebuilding community-based delivery and monitoring of family planning. Of these LGUs, Iloilo City and Pangasinan Province were the first to ask the Family Planning Management Development (FPMD) project for technical assistance to develop a community-based monitoring system that their BSPOs could use for family planning. In 1995, FPMD designed for these two LGUs a simple monitoring scheme for family planning service delivery that BSPOs and other community volunteers can use to record married women of reproductive age, their age, and their health risk

characteristics. It also tracks contraceptive use and nonuse and clearly identifies and prioritizes cases for follow-up. From the one form that the volunteers use, any supervisor at the municipal, district, or city level can consolidate data on users by method, married women of reproductive age, high-risk users, and nonusers, and produce a table for managing service delivery activities and forwarding to the LGU office.

10. *Modified FHSIS, guide for local chief executives and local health personnel in accomplishing forms for the health information system.* Health Intelligence Service. Manila: Department of Health and Department of Interior and Local Government, 1995.

6
Does Decentralization Lead to Better-Quality Services?

Steven Solter

DECENTRALIZING HEALTH SERVICES is a major trend worldwide, with a variety of developing countries trying different models with regard to the speed of implementation and the degree of autonomy allowed to provincial and district health managers. As control over budgets and decision making has shifted to lower levels of the health system, concern has been expressed about the impact on the quality of services being delivered.

One thing is certain about the impact of decentralization on the quality of health services: it is extremely difficult to determine just what that impact is. First, there is the time dimension. Even in situations in which decentralization has been phased in over several years, there has been initial confusion as well as difficulties regarding new roles and responsibilities. This confusion inevitably affects the quality of services being delivered. But since many other variables are also at play (e.g., new local staff are hired; new national policies, other than decentralization, are implemented), it is next to impossible to tease out those factors specifically related to decentralization and to determine to what extent the observed changes in quality of services are owing to decentralization alone.

The difficulty in identifying quality changes secondary to decentralization can be seen in an example from Indonesia during the early 1980s. When the Indonesian Ministry of Health (MOH) decided to experiment with decentralization in three provinces, funds were made available to the provincial health departments to use as they saw fit, subject to minimal restrictions. This experiment lasted for seven years. Even at the end of that time, provincial health officials remained unclear as to what policies they could implement in the province without first receiving Jakarta's blessing. With confusion regarding what was allowable at the provincial level, health staff at the district and subdistrict levels were even more uncertain as to what they could or could not do. What effect all this confusion and uncertainty had on the quality of health services provided by government-sector health facilities (*puskesmas* and *puskesmas pembantu*, which provided the majority of primary health care services) could not be determined with any reliability.

This chapter explores the theoretical connection between quality and decentralization. It then examines what happened when the Philippines decentralized its health system, beginning in 1993. Lessons that can be drawn from the Philippines experience are shared, and the chapter concludes with some final thoughts on the link between quality and decentralization.

Quality and Decentralization: What Is the Connection?

The quality of services provided by primary health care workers can be understood by looking at three different perspectives: the manager's, the health worker's (or health care provider's), and the client's.

A manager is concerned primarily with managing people and systems. The focus is usually on such issues as obtaining adequate staff, funds, and vehicles. In well-managed health programs, managers focus on ensuring that an appropriate range of high-quality services is available to clients seeking those services at a service delivery point. This means that the manager's most important task is to ensure that the provider-client interaction meets the needs of the client and is of high quality. This also means that the manager is managing for results or outcomes rather than for inputs (such as vehicles and staff), which is most often the norm.

The term fully functional service delivery point is used to describe a facility (such as a health center or village health post) that provides the cluster of appropriate services. A service delivery point is fully functional if it has trained staff; a stock of supplies, equipment, and pharmaceuticals; a facility with such basics as running water; a referral system; and information for making decisions. If all these are present, a service delivery point has the *potential* to deliver quality services, but for quality services to actually be delivered, more is necessary. For example, a trained nurse will not provide quality services unless she or he is motivated and receives periodic refresher training (the same is true of doctors and midwives). Similarly, merely having drugs in a clinic does not guarantee that the doctor or nurse will use the drugs in a rational manner. Likewise, the availability of information does not mean that it will be used appropriately for decision making. A critical challenge for primary health care managers is to develop a minimum management package that ensures that service delivery points in their catchment areas are fully functional and deliver quality services. Decentralization by itself does not cause health workers to provide high-quality services. Managers may take advantage of decision-making authority granted by decentralization and make good decisions. Or managers at the local level may actually make things worse by making bad decisions.

Quality from the perspective of health providers often focuses on competence. Health workers want to be competent in what they do and frequently blame the health system for failing to provide the supplies, equipment, and drugs necessary to provide competent or high-quality services.

From the clients' perspective, the main concern is that their needs are met when they interact with the health system or visit a health facility. This often means that they return home with a drug or medicine that the health facility has provided, that they have been treated with respect and consideration, and that they feel that the health provider knew how to treat the presenting problem.

Summing up, there are a number of important functions or factors in a health system that determine quality and are affected by decentralization. Among the most important are:

- training received by health workers (both preservice and in-service)
- health workers' experience
- health workers' motivation
- the drugs, supplies, and equipment, as well as the health facilities available
- the system in which health workers operate (especially the level and quality of supervision, the presence of a functioning referral network, and adequate information and communication for making decisions and informing clients)

Taking each of these factors in turn illustrates some of the issues raised when a health system decentralizes and the quality of health worker and health system performance is assessed.

Training

When training is decentralized, provinces or districts are expected to manage the health worker training system, rather than this being done by the central MOH. The problems that occur at the local level usually have more to do with inexperience than with lack of competence.

To cite the Philippine experience, in-service training of health workers has remained centralized far longer than some other components of the health system. Provinces are only now in the process of taking over responsibility for most in-service training. Some relatively complicated components of training, such as the course for the Integrated Management of Childhood Illness, are still managed by the Department of Health (DOH) in Manila. Other components, such as family planning, are increasingly the responsibility of provinces. When provinces have conducted their own in-service training, they have tended to rely on DOH trainers for assistance, but gradually their self-confidence is increasing and a sustainable training program is becoming possible. The biggest problem is a lack of funds at the provincial or municipal level for training.

Part of the problem is that donors have paid for much of the family planning training in the Philippines. The donors are trying to phase out the funding of training activities, but provinces and cities are reluctant to spend the money themselves. What is needed is for training to become less expensive, with shorter courses held in places where large per diem expenditures are unnecessary. Training can cost less without sacrificing quality, but health staff need to change their level of expectations. For example, they need to participate in more "distance learning" activities, using self-instructional materials; they need to get used to more spartan living accommodations when enrolled in training courses; and they need to expect fewer and shorter in-service courses. If this happens, the quality of training and the skill level of trainees can be maintained at a cost that provinces and municipalities can afford.

Experience

In theory, decentralization should not significantly affect the experience of health workers and the quality of their work. If a doctor, nurse, or midwife has been working for many years, the fact that management of the health system has become the responsibility of a province or district rather than the national government should not make much of a difference. However, decentralization often results in changes in the way health workers carry out their work. For example, a very experienced senior nurse who is responsible for supervising the midwives in her district may be unable to receive a travel allowance as a result of decentralization. She may have been in the habit of visiting rural midwives and traditional birth attendants three times a week. Now she may have to cut off that activity altogether. More experienced and more senior staff may have more difficulty adapting to the changes brought about by decentralization than would younger, less experienced persons. It is difficult to generalize about the impact on quality.

Motivation

Decentralization can have a devastating impact on the quality of care provided by affecting the morale of health care providers. When work conditions are unclear and local officials are perceived as being uninterested in the well-being of health workers, their motivation can plummet and the quality of their work can suffer as a result.

Drugs, Supplies, Equipment, and Health Facilities Infrastructure

Procurement of vital and lifesaving drugs, supplies, and equipment is often devolved to local health officers or other local officials as part of the decentralization process. The obvious advantage is that procurement is managed by people close to the service delivery points who should have a clear idea of what drugs, supplies, and equipment are of the highest priority. Also, decentralized procurement allows local staff to order commodities more quickly to avoid both stockout and overstocking. Since health conditions and health problems can vary tremendously within a diverse country, no single standard package of drugs or supplies is likely to be optimal for every health facility in every province or district.

Centralized procurement, however, has the advantage of being able to utilize economies of scale through bulk purchasing. Huge cost savings are sometimes possible when large quantities of drugs are purchased for nationwide distribution. In addition to cheaper pharmaceuticals, centralized purchasing allows for a wider choice of products, and bribes and kickbacks can be controlled more easily than with local procurement. Also, centralized purchasing usually provides a more rational supply of drugs than does local procurement, where individuals may select drugs without adequate information regarding their efficacy and safety. So which situation leads to higher-quality services—centralized or local procurement?

One solution has been to use centralized procurement for a small number of particularly important and lifesaving drugs to ensure that every health facility has an adequate supply obtained at low cost. For other drugs that may be less essential or for which the demand may vary from place to place, local procurement is preferable. Such a combination of centralized and local procurement, as has been practiced in countries such as Indonesia, has been shown to work well and result in high-quality services.

Supervision, Referral Networks, and Information and Communication

Decentralized health systems in which decisions are made close to where service delivery actually occurs should result in higher-quality services than systems in which decisions are made by bureaucrats living hundreds if not thousands of miles away. Often this is the case. But during the early stages of decentralized decision making, when health managers are not used to making decisions on their own and lack confidence, they may end up postponing decisions or deferring to the MOH, as in pre-decentralization days. It can take time, sometimes years, for local health officials to develop the self-confidence to make key decisions. This is one of the reasons that improvements in service delivery may not be observed until several years after decentralization has been implemented.

Decentralizing Health Services in the Philippines: What Happened to Quality?

The Philippines provides an unusual opportunity to examine what happens to the quality of health services when decentralization takes place. This is true for a number of reasons:

- Decentralization (or devolution, as it is called in the Philippines) of health services occurred rapidly and simultaneously throughout the entire country. If decentralization had been phased in slowly over time or had initially occurred only in selected regions or provinces, its effects would have been different and less dramatic.
- The Philippines is a large country. At the time that decentralization began (1993), the DOH had about 80,000 employees working throughout the archipelago as doctors, nurses, and midwives in hospitals, health centers, rural health units, and *barangay* health stations. With devolution, the

great majority of these health workers and health facilities were devolved to local government units (provinces and municipalities). Such massive changes provide insight into what happens to the quality of service delivery when decentralization occurs.

- The Philippines is an "open" society, with a free press and a population that is free to protest, form unions, and express themselves politically in other ways. Decentralization resulted in a great deal of discussion and political demonstration, so that the views and opinions of health staff affected by devolution were evident.

Decentralization occurred in the Philippines because President Corazon Aquino, elected through the "people power" revolution of 1986, made devolution one of her campaign promises. Because the Philippines is so diverse, with more than 70 million people living in an archipelago of more than 7,000 islands, and has such a great ethnolinguistic variety, it made sense to have more decision-making authority reside in the hands of locally elected officials rather than with bureaucrats or politicians in Manila. Besides, the Marcos dictatorship (1972–86) was a dramatic reminder of the potential abuses of power inherent in a highly centralized system.

The first major step on the road to devolution was passage of the Local Government Code in 1991. The Philippine Congress approved the measure after considerable debate, but the full implications of the law would not be apparent for some time. Health was the most important sector affected; education remained centralized. Health workers and health facilities were to be devolved to local government units (consisting of 75 provinces, 1,526 municipalities, and more than 40,000 *barangays*). Most hospitals and their staffs would be under the direct control of the 75 provincial governors; the great majority of primary health care workers and facilities were devolved to the 1,526 mayors (in the Philippines, each province is divided into about 20 municipalities, including both urban and rural areas, and each municipality is divided into about 25 to 30 *barangays*).

In practice, devolution meant that the great majority of health staff would become employees of mayors at the municipal level. Mayors in the Philippines are elected every three years and typically (especially in rural areas) come from locally powerful and prominent families. Many use their position to reward their political supporters with jobs. Concerns about job security were expressed at an early stage of the devolution process. Many newly devolved doctors, nurses, and midwives were apprehensive about losing their jobs and about being subject to the whims of politicians with little knowledge of or interest in health. The quality of health services provided at the local level was perceived to decline in the early days of devolution (1994–95). One of the reasons was the decrease in motivation due to the fears and anxieties of health staff, who did not believe DOH assurances that there was nothing to worry about. In theory, their jobs were protected through provisions of the Local Government Code. But in practice, health workers knew that Manila-based regulations held little sway in rural areas hundreds of miles away. Where *they* were, the mayor was king.

In addition to the fear of losing their jobs and being replaced by relatives or supporters of the mayor, primary health care workers worried about the difficulties of transferring to other municipalities (which had been easy to do under the predevolution system), loss of their pensions, and loss of other benefits they had received as DOH employees. Rumors of such loss of jobs and benefits spread rapidly throughout the country, and even though many of the rumors were untrue, large numbers of health workers believed them. Some of the stories were true, however. For example, a physician in a rural health unit in Pangasinan Province reported that her mayor required her to be on call 24 hours a day, seven days a week. She interpreted this order as a thinly veiled attempt to force her to resign so that she could be replaced by someone the mayor wanted to reward with a job. (1)

During 1994 and 1995, these fears and anxieties led to mass demonstrations of health workers who were opposed to devolution of health services. Although there is no way of measuring the impact of these concerns on health worker performance or quality, indirect evidence suggests that it was substantial. The highest priority of the DOH at that time was infant immunization (the Expanded Programme on Immunization). After health workers were devolved to provinces and municipalities, there was a significant decline in immunization coverage of infants from approximately 85 percent coverage with the complete series to less than 80 percent. (2) Likewise, the program of high-dose vitamin A capsule distribution to children one to five years of age suffered a decline in coverage levels after devolution began, most likely owing to disruption in service delivery at the local level as well as a significant decline in health worker morale. (3)

One area that clearly impacted quality had to do with local allowances for travel. When employed by the DOH, doctors, nurses, and midwives received a monthly travel allowance to use as they saw fit. Once devolution to the municipalities occurred, this travel allowance was cut off in almost every case. This meant that any travel for supervision of *barangay* health stations, for example, had to be paid out of pocket by the supervisor, instead of being covered by the monthly stipend. This greatly reduced the level of supervision and affected both the morale of *barangay* health station midwives and the distribution of vital drugs, supplies, and equipment. The usual reason given by the mayors for the elimination of travel allowances was that other municipal employees did not receive such allowances. If health workers were paid travel allowances, then all the other municipal workers would demand the same. This, said the mayors, was unacceptable and unaffordable.

Another important component of devolution in the Philippines that greatly affected primary health care delivery was that the provinces were no longer responsible for supporting and supervising the municipalities. Also, the system of district-level supervisors based at district hospitals was eliminated. Under the devolved setup, provincial and district hospitals were the responsibility of the province and were managed by the provincial governors. Specialty and regional hospitals and some large tertiary hospitals were retained by the DOH. Regional offices (the Philippines has 16 regions) were also retained by the DOH. Local health staff were mostly under the authority of the mayors, except for a relatively small number retained by the DOH so that it could have representation on local health boards. In practice, this meant that governors and provincial health staff became involved with managing hospitals and no longer took much responsibility for or interest in what happened in the municipalities. This was understandable, given that the governors rarely had enough money to cover the operational costs of running the hospitals. District hospitals, which formerly served as the nucleus of district teams that supervised adjacent municipalities, no longer had any connection with the municipalities and ceased their support and supervisory activities. Some provinces were greatly affected by these changes. For example, Cebu, Pangasinan, and Negros Occidental Provinces contained at least 40 municipalities each. Now that the provincial health offices focused on hospitals and the district teams no longer visited municipalities, the mayors and the municipalities were on their own. They got little help regarding quality assurance.

Despite all the problems and difficulties enumerated above, the DOH was able to take a number of steps that reduced the level of confusion and disruption brought about by the sudden transfer of authority and responsibility to local officials. For example, in 1993 the DOH began a series of highly publicized national campaigns to eradicate polio, expand overall immunization coverage, and provide high-dose vitamin A capsules. These campaigns (National Immunization Days and National Nutrition Days) were very successful and helped compensate for some of the problems and dislocations at the local level caused by devolution.

The DOH needed to make a number of radical changes in its role vis-à-vis the provinces and municipalities. However, once health services devolved to the Local Government Units, most DOH officials based in Manila or in the regional offices continued to act as if nothing had changed. Instead of transforming itself into an organization responsible for *managing* the delivery of preventive, promotive, and curative health services by setting policy, establishing quality standards, issuing regulations, and accrediting health facilities, the DOH continued to behave as if it were still in the business of *directly providing* health services at the primary health care level. At the same time, health officials at the provincial and municipal levels continued to behave as if the status quo had not changed. Only when it became clear that sufficient operating funds from the central government would not be forthcoming did local health officials realize that the world had changed and that they had to do something about it.

Lessons Learned from the Philippine Experience

Among the major lessons learned to date are the following:

- The most important lesson is that decentralization must be planned and the implications thoroughly understood before the process begins. This is especially important if, as was the case in the Philippines, decentralization is rapid, comprehensive, and nationwide.
- Another critical lesson for maintaining quality at the service delivery level is that it is just as important for central-level health officials to change their roles and styles as it is for local-level health officials to change. Decentralization efforts often fail because local-level changes are overemphasized and the equally important central-level changes are neglected.
- A third lesson is that once decentralization has occurred, frontline health workers must feel confident about job security and job benefits. Without this confidence, morale suffers, as do job performance and the quality of the work performed.
- A relatively simple thing—such as eliminating a small monthly travel allowance to enable health staff to go on supervisory visits without incurring out-of-pocket costs—can have an enormous and devastating impact on quality. In the Philippines today, if you ask municipal health officers how devolution has affected the quality of health services, they reveal that abolishing travel allowances has practically stopped supervisory visits, and that without supervision, the quality of service will inevitably decline.

Conclusions

Decentralization is difficult, but it can lead to a more democratic system in which local people control the major decisions affecting their lives. Quantitative evidence linking decentralization and quality is lacking, however. Case studies and close observation can help clarify the connections, but given the complexity of the variables involved, no study is likely to be carried out that will definitively answer the questions raised in this chapter.

Efforts are under way (see chapter 5) to certify health facilities in the Philippines as having met predefined quality standards. Certification programs of this sort, however, cannot tell us what the quality of services would have been had devolution not taken place.

If it is so difficult, if not impossible, to describe the cause-and-effect relationship between the decentralization of primary health care services in developing countries and the quality of service delivery, what can we say about this issue? First, decentralization clearly affects the quality of service delivery in primary health care, but whether the impact in the long run is positive or negative must be judged on a case-by-case basis. The empirical evidence thus far does not lead to any easy generalization. Second, the usual trend is for service quality to decline in the initial stages of decentralization and then gradually improve once roles and responsibilities are sorted out. In some cases, the quality of care has not yet returned to the level it was before decentralization. Finally, in most cases in which health workers have been employed by a centralized MOH (for example, working at a rural health center as an employee of the MOH) and then devolved to the local level, their morale has suffered because of the perception that their new job situations are less secure.

References

1. Personal communication, September 1994.
2. Estimates of immunization coverage come from two main sources:

routinely reported service statistics and special coverage surveys. The numbers provided here represent the best available estimate from the Maternal and Child Health Service, DOH, covering 1993 and 1994.

3. Vitamin A capsule distribution coverage relies on the same data sets as for infant immunization.

PART II

Health Services

7

Implementation and Integration of Reproductive Health Services in a Decentralized System

Iain W. Aitken

DECENTRALIZATION AND GREATER ATTENTION to reproductive health care are two key changes that have affected health services in the 1990s. The decision to decentralize has generally been a political one. In a few cases, it has been an intentional and well-considered aspect of health-sector reform, but usually its implementation in the health sector follows political changes, and health services organizations have had to adapt to the new decentralized structures as best they could. The commitment to the new policies on reproductive health, undertaken at the International Conference on Population and Development (ICPD) in Cairo in 1994, also involves significant changes in and reorganization of health services. For many people around the world, some of these policies are controversial. Their implementation involves the introduction of new programs, the integration of previously separate activities, and the acquisition of new skills by many health professionals. The purpose of this chapter is to consider both the process and the goals of the changes required by the implementation of reproductive health services and to assess the extent to which they are compatible or in conflict with those of decentralization.

Reproductive Health

In its 1993 *World Development Report*, (1) the World Bank estimated that 34 percent of the burden of disease for women of reproductive age in developing countries is due to reproductive health problems, and 19 percent of the burden of disease for children under five years of age is from perinatal causes. Reproductive health problems account for 28 percent of the burden of disease for women in Asia but 60 percent of the burden of disease for women in Africa. It is hardly surprising, therefore, that prenatal and delivery care, treatment of sexually transmitted diseases (STDs), and family planning are all included in the minimum essential package of clinical services recommended in the *World Development Report*.

The Programme of Action adopted by 184 member states attending the ICPD in Cairo endorsed a new strategy for addressing population issues. This strategy is intended to meet the individual needs of women and men rather than to achieve the demographic targets that characterized the approach of the previous 20 years. (2) Adapting the World Health Organization (WHO) definition of health, the Cairo program defines reproductive health as (2)

> a state of complete physical, mental and social well-being and ... not merely the absence of disease or infirmity, in all matters relating to the reproductive system and to its functions and processes. Reproductive health therefore implies that people are able to have a satisfying and safe sex life and that they have the capability to reproduce and the freedom to decide if, when and how often to do so. Implicit in this last condition are the right of men and women to be informed about and to have access to safe, effective, affordable and acceptable methods of family planning of their choice, as well as other methods of their choice for regulation of fertility which are not against the law, and the right of access to appropriate health-care services that will enable women to go safely through pregnancy and childbirth and provide couples with the best chance of having a healthy infant. (para. 7.2)

In adopting this program, governments undertook to reduce 1990 maternal mortality levels by one-half by the year 2000 and by a further one-half by the year 2015. The program also recognizes unsafe abortion as a leading cause of maternal mortality and as a major public health concern. It commits to the prevention of STDs—including the human immune deficiency virus (HIV) and acquired immune deficiency syndrome (AIDS)—and to the provision of services to treat and counsel those who are infected. Under the program, states agree to

> take steps to meet family planning needs of their populations as soon as possible and should, in all cases by the year 2015, seek to provide universal access to a full range of safe and reliable family planning methods and to related reproductive health services which are not against the law. (para. 7.16)

In addition to these activities and targets for the health sector, the program commits itself to the eradication of female genital mutilation, universal primary school education by the year 2015, and the introduction of appropriate sex education in schools.

A comparison of these targets with only a few of the statistics on the current state of women's reproductive health makes it clear that this is an ambitious program. Each year approximately 600,000 women die during pregnancy or in association with childbirth. Almost 99 percent of these women live in developing countries, where the lifetime chance of maternal death is 1 in 20, compared with 1 in 4,000 in industrialized countries. (3) In part this reflects marginal states of nutrition and general health; 56 percent of women in the developing world are anemic during pregnancy. (4) Although the means for correcting this situation are available, only 65 percent of these women receive any antenatal care, and many of those who do are seen only once or twice, so that minimal effective benefit is gained. (5) The main reason, however, that women die in association with pregnancy and childbirth is that when complications do arise, women have inadequate access to lifesaving care. Only 53 percent of women in developing countries have a skilled attendant at delivery, and only 40 percent actually deliver in a health facility. (5) Although more emergency obstetric skills could be delegated to health center staff, (6) their skills and facilities are limited, and most women requiring emergency attention need referral to a district hospital. It is the failure of this referral system, for a variety of reasons, that accounts for the high maternal mortality rates. (7) The failure to care for women during pregnancy and childbirth also accounts for the continuing high perinatal mortality rates. These cases constitute the resistant portion of infant mortality, which has been largely untouched by the otherwise effective child survival interventions of the past 20 years.

Each year, there are about 55 million induced abortions worldwide. About half of these are done under unsafe conditions, leading to an estimated 60,000 to 100,000 deaths. (8) As with other causes of maternal death, the fatalities result from delayed or no access to the appropriate level of care. Many of the deaths could be avoided by access to health workers and facilities capable of performing safe abortions, but even in countries such as India, where abortion is legal, the same barriers and delays apply that limit the effectiveness of emergency obstetric care. Many abortions and many high-risk pregnancies could have been avoided by the use of effective contraception, but many couples are prevented from using effective modern methods by lack of information or access or by socioeconomic barriers. In developing countries (excluding China), only 36 percent of women of reproductive age are using modern methods of contraception. In Africa, the proportion is only 18 percent. (9)

STDs are becoming increasingly prevalent worldwide. WHO estimates an annual incidence of STDs of more than 250 million and expects the incidence of HIV to be more than 26 million by the year 2000. (10) Women bear the greatest burden of disease from STDs, both because of the greater efficiency of male-to-female transmission and because the majority of these infections in women are asymptomatic and therefore remain untreated. In many parts of Africa, the complications of STDs and other reproductive tract infections account for about 85 percent of all female causes of infertility. (11) Infertility always has personal costs, but in many parts of the world it also carries the high social costs of stigma and divorce.

Decentralization

Decentralization is being implemented in an increasing number of countries at this time and takes a number of different forms. In Nicaragua, this meant *deconcentration*, the transfer of authority and responsibility to the integrated local health systems, lower levels within the government health system. In the Philippines, power over the health services has been *devolved* to provincial, city, and municipal governments that are separate from the central Ministry of Health. In other countries there is a mixed form of decentralization. In Nigeria, responsibility for hospitals was deconcentrated to the states, and power over primary health care and family planning was devolved to the local government authorities. In Chile, both hospitals and public health programs were deconcentrated to autonomous health service areas, and basic health services were devolved to municipalities. Decentralization may thus affect the health sector alone, several ministries, or most aspects of government. The key elements of government power that are transferred in this way include decisions about budgets and human resources.

The advantages of decentralization include:

- local "ownership" of and accountability for government programs
- responsiveness to local needs
- efficient management of resources
- management information systems and supervision linked to local planning and management of programs
- easier interagency coordination (12)

Many of these benefits have been realized equally well in situations of deconcentration as in those of devolution of power.

These two sets of policies, reproductive health and decentralization, appear to be compatible when attempts are made to adopt and implement them. Both involve notions of human rights and democratization and share the goal of improving human development in efficient and acceptable ways. There is little documentation of the implementation of either decentralization of health services or reproductive health policies to date, and even less of the two together. Experience from a number of countries, however, suggests that the implementation of these two policies is complex and that decentralization may not always facilitate realization of the Cairo reproductive health agenda.

Reproductive Health Policy-Making and Decentralization

Policies in support of women's health and women's rights have been adopted at the country level and at the international level because of the work of feminists and feminist organizations. In most situations, these have met with considerable opposition from conservative religious and political bodies. Decentralization increases the number of people and institutions involved in policy formulation, and reproductive health policies have been promoted and opposed at both central and peripheral levels of government. The problem inherent to decentralization for those promoting a reproductive health agenda may be in the large number of local government bodies that need to be persuaded in some countries.

In 1983, feminists in São Paulo, Brazil, brought about the formation of a State Council for Women's Rights under the state government. Two years later that led to the formation of a National Council for Women's Rights by congressional law under the Ministry of Justice. Its mandate was broad and included reproductive health, domestic violence, labor, the status of rural women, and women's education. By 1989, there were 34 councils at the state or municipal levels. Also in 1983, a group of women's health activists initiated discussions in the Ministry of Health that led to the creation of the Program of Integral Assistance to Women's Health. Its aims were to increase the coverage and quality of prenatal and delivery care, expand services for the control of breast and cervical cancer, promote family planning, and diagnose and treat STDs and infertility. This represented the first true involvement of the state in women's health and encouraged expansion of collaboration between the family planning association, BEMFAM, and the municipalities until over 25 percent of the 4,450 municipalities were involved. (13), (14)

In Mexico, the big women's health issue has been abortion. In 1976, the Coalition of Feminist Women was formed at the national level to pursue liberalization of the law against abortion. There were no results until 1990, when the congress of the state of Chiapas passed a law decriminalizing abortions done in the first 90 days of gestation for family planning reasons. The responses from Pro Vida, the Catholic Church, and the conservative National Action Party (PAN) were immediate, and the state congress revoked the law. (15) Since then, PAN has won several state governorships, and in states such as Chihuahua, where they held a majority in the congress, they even managed to change the local constitution to include "the right to life from the moment of conception," even though it contravened the federal constitution and state penal codes. (16)

National policies may fail to be implemented at the local government level for a number of reasons. In the Philippines, a newly appointed provincial governor stopped the implementation of a US Agency for International Development (USAID)–funded health project in his province because he opposed the family planning component. (17) In Colombia, a National Women's Health Policy was passed in 1992 under a sympathetic minister, but three years later there was still no action because no funds had been budgeted at the state level. (18) More recently, as part of the Colombian health-sector reform, new agencies called Empresas Promotoras de Salud (EPSs) have been made responsible for the purchase of health services for individuals. Because the law did not specify which family planning services were to be covered by the new health plan, the EPSs decided that contraceptives were not preventive health measures and have been unwilling to cover them. (19)

The most resistant barriers to the successful initiation of new reproductive health programs are likely to be the innate conservatism and resistance to change of the health workers and health systems themselves. For example, there may be a culture-based reluctance to provide services to adolescents or women with incomplete abortions. For similar reasons there may be unwillingness to acknowledge the possibility of STDs among one population of women while harboring a judgmental attitude toward its evident prevalence among women of another socioeconomic group. Aside from attitudinal problems, the extra work and redesign of programs alone may be enough to create resistance.

Implementation of Reproductive Health Programs

The goals of reproductive and sexual health services in most countries are to expand access to and enhance the quality of family planning services, STD and HIV prevention and control, safe motherhood and postabortion care, and, in some countries, legal and safe induced abortion services. There are three main complementary approaches to achieving these goals: improving the client-provider interface, developing functioning health systems, and integrating reproductive health services.

Improving the Client-Provider Interface

Accessibility and quality of care in reproductive health services have received a lot of attention in recent years. (20), (21) The low utilization rates of family planning and maternity services and the inadequacy of many STD services relate to combinations of the following factors: low health worker density, deficient technical skills, poor human relations skills and attitudes, and inadequate or faulty equipment and supplies. (22), (23) Satisfactory progress in improving access and quality will depend on improving performance in all four aspects of the delivery system. These, in turn, depend on the amount and control of other resources and government functions, all of which may be adversely affected by the process and existence of decentralization.

FINANCIAL ALLOCATIONS AND RESOURCES. Equity is a frequent casualty of the process of decentralization. Most countries have regions with more resources and a better local tax base than others. These regions can usually attract the more able professionals and managers into their governments, who in turn are able to attract or generate more resources and run a more efficient organization. Health services in poorer areas are at the mercy of the resources available to the central government and the priorities of the local government or administration. In Nigeria, for example, less than 20 percent of public health facilities had family planning supplies in 1994, and the oral pills that were the most commonly used method were usually purchased from private sources. (24)

In many countries, financial allocations to local governments from the central government are made on a strict per capita basis. In others, allocations are weighted in favor of less well developed regions, which can ameliorate but usually not remove the inequities. Weighting needs to take into account a number of issues, balancing short-term and long-term needs. For example, in Bolivia, where the municipalities are small, the initial simple per capita formula that was used failed to take into account the nature of the health services that were already established in the local government regions. As a consequence, those with the more expensive tertiary referral hospitals found themselves short of funds. Weighting in favor of less well developed regions is generally required not for immediate running costs but for infrastructure and program development.

Nongovernmental organizations (NGOs) may become vulnerable in a decentralized situation if they are dependent on government subsidies. In Papua New Guinea, about 50 percent of rural health services are provided by church-related health facilities. In the mid-1970s, both government and church health services were rationalized to maximize coverage of the population. Church institutions received government subsidies based on the size of population they served. Following decentralization, new contracts had to be made between the provincial governments and the church health authorities. In the late 1980s, there was a series of budget cuts for the health sector, as a result of which several provincial governments reduced or stopped their payments to the churches. Several churches were forced to withdraw from operating health services. (25)

HUMAN RESOURCES FOR HEALTH. Human resources are the key to any health program, and salaries and benefits constitute the bulk of most health care budgets. A key decision in the process of decentralization is therefore whether to retain or decentralize a national public service system. Retention maintains a core stability in the health system but may restrict the ability of local governments to innovate. In practice, however, wealthier local governments can usually get more positions created by the public service commission and develop their programs the way they want. This may not create problems when the supply of health workers is adequate. But when there are scarce supplies, as in Papua New Guinea, a wealthy local government may be able to add local salary bonuses or other perquisites to attract good people for the positions, and thus bias the national distribution of specialized human resources required for improving reproductive health services.

Transfer of staff from a central public service to local governments has been associated with a loss of benefits for the health workers in both the Philippines and Zambia. (17) Changes in salary levels, inadequate funding of local health programs, and politicization of local appointments have increased the level of uncertainty and adversely affected health staff morale, resulting in deterioration in the quality of care.

An adequate supply of the right kinds of reproductive health workers depends on basic information about their demand, supply, and loss from the workforce. It also requires sufficiently funded training programs. When a national public service is disbanded and all employment becomes the prerogative of local governments, the information systems may rapidly break down. If responsibility for training programs has also been turned over to local governments, inadequate funding can quickly lead to the closing of training schools. (26)

Continuing education programs have also suffered from both a lack of funds and, where local government units are small, a lack of professional technical capacity to provide such continuing education. Sometimes, as happened in the Philippines, local managers may be unwilling to release health workers to attend courses that are arranged through a national or regional administration. Such constraints are obviously significant when job revision and development are required to meet the needs of a new reproductive health program. Complaints about uncoordinated training from the periphery are sometimes legitimate; in Papua New Guinea, the provincial health officers insisted on having more input into the scheduling and coordination of centrally organized courses so that their workers would have time to do some work.

PROCUREMENT OF DRUGS AND SUPPLIES. The purchasing of drugs and supplies may be decentralized, or the central government may retain its central drug purchasing and distribution agency. When procurement has been decentralized, shortages of medical supplies may occur. The local government may have inadequate funds to buy the quantities required, as occurred in some municipalities in the Philippines, or there may be delays in the disbursement of funds by the local government, as happened in Bolivia. Costs of drugs, contraceptives, equipment, and supplies are sensitive to economies of scale, which may make all the difference in the affordability and therefore sustainability of a family planning program designed to reach poor people. This issue depends to a large extent on the size of the populations of the decentralized political entities and argues for more centralized procurement. Quality control and the registration of drugs are other areas that are better managed by a central government agency. The central government or professional associations can also be the means for developing a consensus about standard management regimens and essential drug lists and can provide appropriate guidance to those responsible for procurement, whether at the central or local government level.

Developing Functioning Health Systems

The advantages of decentralization ought to be seen in the development of more effective and efficient health systems. The freedom to respond to the particularities of a local situation and to develop appropriate health systems is one of the main arguments for decentralization. The reality, however, may prove to be very different, depending on how decentralization is designed and implemented and the maturity of the health systems involved.

VERTICAL INTEGRATION OF HEALTH PROGRAMS. Under decentralization, there is a great potential for improving vertical integration within health programs, integrating hospital, health center, and community-level services as well as referral and transport systems. Achievement of this integration is necessary for the implementation of an adequate safe motherhood program. (27) It is also necessary for the provision of effective choice between nonclinical contraceptives, provided at the community level, and the clinical methods that are usually available only at health centers or hospitals.

Many of the gains inherent in the principle of integration were obtained through the promotion of district health systems, prior to the implementation of full decentralization. (28) In Papua New Guinea, as part of the 1974–78 Health Plan, each province maintained one provincial hospital as the referral hospital for all government and nongovernment health centers and village aid posts. During the 1980s, many provinces installed radios at health centers to facilitate consultation and referral. The impact on maternal health was limited by the levels of institutional deliveries and the usual problems of transportation, but in general, the referral and supervision system worked. (29) The introduction of decentralization made little difference to the overall structure and functioning of the health system in Papua New Guinea, and subsequent changes in outputs and impacts of the system were more the result of changes in administration and resource fluctuations. (30)

Urban areas often have the opposite problems from rural areas; major hospitals tend to be overused by patients who do not require such sophisticated facilities. An excellent example is provided by the Lusaka Urban Maternity Project in Zambia. There, the pressure on an overcrowded university maternity hospital and an overworked staff was relieved by the creation of a number of low-risk maternity centers in the urban health centers of the city, all managed as part of a unitary system of referral and supervision. (31)

In reality, the decentralized district health system does not always work out as hoped. After decentralization in Papua New Guinea, conflicts arose between some provincial health officers and the medical superintendents of their provincial hospitals because the medical superintendents perceived themselves to be more highly qualified. The same situation in Nicaragua actually led to withdrawal of the five main hospitals into independent jurisdictions. In the Philippines, Zambia, and Bolivia, previously well-developed systems of integrated regional and district health administrations were broken up by decentralization, so that referral hospitals are often in different local government areas from primary care services. In Bolivia, a recently introduced health insurance program provides coverage for normal and complicated deliveries as well as some child health services. There is, however, no mechanism for transferring funds between municipalities to reimburse referral hospitals for services provided to women from other municipalities.

HEALTH PROGRAM MANAGEMENT. Management breakdowns and inadequacies have been among the most visible problems resulting from decentralization, but they are neither ubiquitous nor inevitable. There is evidence that decentralized population and family planning programs in Anglophone Africa and elsewhere have benefited from the additional freedom to respond to local cultural needs, mobilize local resources, and thereby expand into previously underserved communities. (32) In Malaysia, since the early 1990s, budget allocation has been decentralized and a program of management training provided for district health teams. In this already well-developed and well-funded health system, the results have included redistribution of health staff to areas of need, pooling of resources, improved collection and utilization of health information in planning and monitoring, strengthening of health promotion in collaboration with NGOs, and greater involvement of communities in health services. (33)

Many management problems arise when authority is transferred to government levels that have previously had little or no management responsibility for technical activities such as health or education, or when decentralization happens with little or no preparation. New organizational and management structures, systems, and procedures need to be designed and implemented, and people need to be trained for their new management roles. Success or failure largely depends on how quickly the process of decentralization is implemented. In Ghana, decentralization is being phased in over several years, allowing for the development and trial of new systems and the training of staff for new roles. In Papua New Guinea, an immediate crisis was averted because government was decentralized to the provincial secretariats and health offices, which had previously exercised considerable administrative powers. Problems emerged later as provincial health staff grappled with larger management issues in increasingly political environments. (29) In the Philippines, Zambia, and Bolivia, many of the more rural municipalities had little or no experience of local government or management and had to create new secretariats. Some of the Bolivian municipalities were so small that they had to merge with adjacent municipalities to create a viable entity. Health planning requires people's time and skills. In Brazil, many of the smaller municipalities lacked not only training programs in planning and management but also sufficient money to start a planning process. (34)

Where resources are scarce, new health problems and challenges, such as reproductive health, are particularly threatened under a decentralized system. Technical and management skills that have been developed to maintain familiar programs may be inadequate to deal with these new public health issues. In many parts of Africa, district health authorities that have succeeded in taking advantage of decentralization to improve family planning and maternal and child health services have faced considerable difficulties in responding to the HIV/AIDS epidemic. Lack of access to up-to-date scientific information and inadequate training budgets prevent program and professional development; lack of a relevant information system constrains intelligent management of the program; and unstable donor aid leads to inconsistent government funding priorities and, therefore, unpredictable funding for the program. (35) Similar problems occurred in the 1980s in Papua New Guinea at the time of decentralization. Increasing mobility of the population was leading to rapid spread of STDs and tuberculosis from urban areas to rural and remote communities; these diseases were taking on epidemic proportions in the cities. The emergence of nongonococcal urethritis and drug resistance required considerably more complicated approaches to diagnosis and management. Many of the provincial health authorities were neither technically nor managerially prepared for these changes. Furthermore, declining health budgets made it almost impossible to invest resources in expanded training and control programs. (29) It is precisely in situations like this that local government officials rely on technical support and guidance from the central government or from aid project personnel. When one central ministry makes decisions on policy and program design, the dissemination of technical standards and advice is not too complicated. When several hundred local government units have to be informed and persuaded about new policies and programs or wish to contribute to the formulation of policy, the situation becomes both complex and expensive because of all the travel and communications required.

Most management systems need change or modification under decentralization. One that frequently needs radical reconceptualizing is the health management information system. Health information systems are frequently designed to provide information to central program managers, whose management and planning time frame is usually measured in years. Decentralization demands the adaptation of these information systems to meet the management needs of those at the local level who are responsible for supervising and managing the various reproductive health services. Such data become the necessary basis for strategic planning and budgeting at the local level. But they should also provide the means for monitoring, month by month, the progress of programs in different communities so that problems can be identified and solved. (36)

COMMUNITY PARTICIPATION. Finally, decentralization can create opportunities for more direct involvement of constituents and communities. A good example is the Local Initiatives Program, which has been helping to improve the performance of the Bangladesh Family Planning Program at the community level. The Local Initiatives Program works with 36,000 women volunteers who supply pills and condoms in their communities and refer clients for clinical services. The key strategy is the creation of management teams at the subdistrict level, consisting of family planning, health, development, and local government officers and community-level management teams with community participants. The program covers a quarter of the country's population and has raised the contraceptive prevalence rate for modern methods to 65 percent, compared with 41.5 percent in other areas. (37)

Integrating Reproductive Health Services

The concept of reproductive health requires a perspective that not only includes safe motherhood, STD control, and population and family planning programs but also envisions them as being much more organically integrated. The idea of integration has been around for a long time, but up to now, the motivation has clearly been the promotion of family planning. (38, 39) Now that the primary goal is the reproductive health of women and men, the objectives and methods of integration need to be reconsidered. Three more appropriate objectives are safety, synergy between programs, and social convenience for clients. The relative importance of these three objectives, as well as the ways of achieving them, will vary from place to place.

MOTIVES AND METHODS FOR SERVICE INTEGRATION. The HIV pandemic has created an awareness of the concurrent problems of other STDs such as syphilis, gonorrhea, and *Chlamydia trachomatis*. Pregnancy and childbirth are associated with vertical transmission of these diseases from mother to child. Pregnancy, childbirth, abortion, and the use of certain contraceptives may all lead to an increased incidence of pelvic inflammatory disease and infertility. The first goal of integration of reproductive health services must therefore be safety. The goal of safety is served by integrating into prenatal care clinics screening for syphilis, (40) possibly gonorrhea and chlamydia, (41) and HIV where resources for treatment are adequate. (42) The insertion of intrauterine devices (IUDs) is associated with an increased risk of pelvic inflammatory disease, particularly in the presence of gonorrhea and chlamydial infections. (43) When IUDs are among the contraceptives offered in a family planning clinic, laboratory tests or the "syndromic" approach (44) should be used to screen for these infections, or prophylactic treatment should be given.

The integration of two different reproductive health services can increase the coverage or effectiveness of either one or both of those services. The goal here is synergy. There is clearly an overlap of safety concerns when primary prevention of STDs, including HIV, is integrated with family planning services. This would promote a greater awareness of STDs and their prevention as well as the use of condoms. MEXFAM and PROFAMILIA, private family planning organizations in Mexico and Colombia, both successfully incorporated AIDS prevention messages into their community marketing and media programs without negatively impacting the family planning programs. (45, 46) Family planning can also be promoted through counseling during prenatal care and the provision of contraceptives in association with postnatal care or child health clinics, as demonstrated in Tunisia (47) and Mexico. (48) Another example of horizontal integration of services at the same level, often by the same health worker, is the provision of contraceptive services after pregnancy termination. Studies in India and Bangladesh have found that women are receptive to family planning after an abortion and have demonstrated that it is highly cost-effective to provide contraception at that time. (49, 50)

Safety and synergy are goals that arise primarily from the public health concerns of providers. Integration that creates greater social convenience for community members contributes to the other goal identified at the Cairo ICPD—women's empowerment. (51) In many countries, women have to go to different facilities or even different organizations for prenatal care and family planning, or they may go to the same clinic building for prenatal care and health care for their children but on different days of the week. (23) Locating the different services in one facility and making them available at the same time reinforce the goals of safety and synergy and create the convenience of "one-stop shopping" for services. It also increases the possibility of privacy, such as when a woman may not want others to know what services she is seeking by obviously going to the family planning clinic or the prenatal clinic.

Safety, synergy, and social convenience, the three objectives of integrating reproductive health services, all imply organizational changes in the way health care is delivered. Some may have profound institutional and interinstitutional implications, which are discussed later. The first issue is what these three goals imply for the organization of service delivery. Do they require expanded roles for health workers, the creation of teams of workers performing different tasks or functions in the same facility, or referral systems between facilities? In most situations, the incorporation of screening for STDs into prenatal care and family planning clinics requires expansion of the roles of the health workers. The need for safety in pregnancy and contraception implies that information gained from screening be used in the immediate provision of appropriate prenatal and contraceptive care. As important as this is, implementation is not necessarily easy.

Nurses and midwives working in prenatal care and family planning clinics are usually not used to dealing with STDs. Therefore, new skills have to be learned and new activities incorporated into the clinic timetable. This will probably increase the time spent with each client. Perhaps most importantly, the health workers have to overcome their reluctance to talk with their clients about genital symptoms and sexual behaviors. Special training programs were designed by NGOs in Bangladesh to help clinic workers overcome their feelings of shame and develop confidence about speaking of such things.

The benefits of synergy can be achieved both by expanded health worker roles and by team building. Horizontal integration between family planning and STD prevention, and the promotion of family planning during and after pregnancy, can best be achieved by including these tasks in the same health worker's activities. However, a lot can still be achieved when one person promotes family planning in the context of a child health clinic but the actual counseling and provision of contraceptives are done by a different health worker on the same day in another room in the same facility. This is also a good example of reaching the goal of social convenience, allowing a woman to attend to her child's immunization needs and her contraceptive needs during the same clinic visit.

The advantages of expanding the roles of health workers have to be offset against the problems of job overload. Sometimes there may be too many clients to serve, or the number and diversity of tasks and activities mean that some tasks get done and others receive much less or no attention. (52) In a decentralized system, it is possible for local health authorities to use human resources to their best advantage, depending on the availability of different types of health workers and the local pattern of health problems.

ADMINISTRATIVE INTEGRATION. Integration of reproductive health programs at the administrative level introduces issues that are much less clear than those of service integration. In the past, population and family planning programs were sometimes set in their own government ministry, separate from the health ministry. Attempts at subsequent reintegration have met with differing degrees of success. In Malaysia, the integration of two institutions that were already well managed was accomplished over several years. (53) In Bangladesh, the family planning program originally functioned under an interministerial board but was later integrated into the Ministry of Health. Because of difficulties encountered in the process of integration, the family planning program still operates with its own budget, personnel system, and chain of command within the health ministry. However, there has been an attempt to achieve some real integration at the subdistrict level by placing a health administrator from the health division in charge of all curative, preventive, and family planning services in the area. This achieves reasonable functional integration between family planning and maternal and child health services most of the time but does little to ameliorate the entrenched interests of two otherwise independent administrations. (39) In the Philippines, family planning services that had previously come under the Population Commission were transferred to the Ministry of Health. As such, they have now been decentralized to local governments. The Population Commission retained all promotional activities for population concerns but remained a centralized body, making integration of promotion and service delivery more difficult. (17)

In Kenya in 1983, the government adopted its District Focus for Rural Development Policy, which has led to increasingly deconcentrated administration of many government functions. In 1982, the National Council for Population and Development was created to oversee all population-related activities and currently comes under the Ministry of Planning and National Development. Under the decentralized system, the District Population Officer (DPO) is supposed to coordinate all family planning and other population activities at the district level. In practice, there were delays in filling the positions. In those districts where there was a DPO, the relationship with the district health officer was often strained because the health officer was responsible for all the government health workers who were providing family planning services. As a consequence, a tacit division of responsibilities developed, and the DPOs spent most of their time working with NGOs that were promoting family planning. This resulted in overlapping and competing community-based contraceptive delivery systems in many areas and a total lack of coordination with the government health staff providing clinical contraceptive methods at health centers. (24)

BEMFAM in Brazil is a good example of successful administrative integration of decentralized local governments and an NGO. The municipality provides facilities, staff, and some money, and BEMFAM provides training, contraceptive supplies, supervision, and technical support. Planning for local expansion and development of the program is a joint activity. This model has been successfully adopted by more than a thousand municipalities in Brazil. (14)

There is still too little information about attempts to accomplish integration of reproductive health services at the same time as or following decentralization. In theory, decentralization should provide an organizational structure that supports attempts to integrate services, but in practice, individuals in the system may not be supportive of either decentralization or integration. An attempt by the King of Nepal to integrate family planning into the health ministry and later to decentralize the health services package met with considerable resistance from senior staff of the family planning program. Objections were primarily due to the lack of permanent posts, the failure of a number of skilled employees to qualify for permanent posts, and the consequent loss of status and authority they suffered. (54) Success therefore depends on the willingness and ability of the professionals and functionaries within the central administration to fully and competently change from their original roles of managers to national policy makers and technical advisers to local governments. This change is very difficult. In Papua New Guinea, because of the resistance of senior officers in the Ministry of Health, it took four years and the replacement of the chief executive in the ministry before the changes mandated by the Organic Law on Provincial Government were even begun to be implemented. (55) Even after the complete replacement of senior officers, the new people in these posts did not always find the technical adviser role easy to assume. They had been promoted from managerial positions and did not necessarily have much more technical expertise than their provincial counterparts.

Conclusions

The Programme of Action of the Cairo ICPD, which promotes a reproductive health approach to population and development, is a challenge to all the countries that adopted it. Many of those countries are also embarked on some version of health-sector reform that includes the decentralization of government or health services administration. Decentralization has both advantages and disadvantages for the achievement of the Programme of Action. One main advantage is the possibility of the application and further development of the district health system approach. This encourages community participation as well as vertical integration between primary care services and the district hospital. It allows flexibility in the integration of the different components of reproductive health in a way that best suits local needs and resources. It provides the stimulus for the development of management systems appropriate to the needs of an administration at that level.

Decentralization can also hinder implementation of the reproductive health approach. Problems can arise from the way in which decentralization is designed and implemented. First, because it is usually politically motivated, the design of decentralization does not necessarily take note of the consequences for complex ministries, such as the health ministry. The local government units in many countries are much too small for the development of a district health system, making referrals difficult, health financing complex, and the coordination of health promotion and disease control programs ineffective. Other problems include the changing roles of health administrators at the center and periphery, requiring both changed attitudes and considerable training inputs; possible policy conflicts between the center and periphery; increasing inequities among different parts of the country; and breakdowns in both the supply and the motivation of health staff through mismanagement of training programs and conditions of service. The haste and the lack of due consideration given to the process of planning and implementation in many countries are perhaps the main reasons why many of these problems have occurred. Countries that succeed in developing good-quality reproductive health programs are noteworthy both for their commitment to the values expressed in the Cairo Programme of Action and for the time and care taken to design and implement processes of integration and decentralization.

References

1. World Bank. *World development report 1993: Investing in health*. New York: Oxford University Press, 1993, pp. 117, 216.
2. United Nations. *Report of the International Conference on Population and Development*. Document A/Conf. 171/13. New York: UN, 1994.
3. World Health Organization and UNICEF. *Revised 1990 estimates of maternal mortality: A new approach by WHO and UNICEF*. Geneva: WHO, 1996.
4. World Health Organization. *The prevalence of anemia in women*. WHO/MCH/92.2. Geneva: WHO, 1992.
5. World Health Organization. *Coverage of maternity care*. WHO/RHT/MSM/96.28. Geneva: WHO, 1996.
6. Aitken, I. W. The feasibility of decentralizing essential obstetric care to peripheral facilities. In: D. M. Measham, ed. *Issues in essential obstetric care*. Report of a technical meeting of the Inter-Agency Group for

Safe Motherhood, May 31–June 2, 1995. New York: Population Council and Family Care International, 1996.
7. Thaddeus, S., and D. Maine. *Too far to walk: Maternal mortality in context*. New York: Prevention of Maternal Mortality Program, Center for Population and Family Health, Columbia University, 1990.
8. World Bank, *World development report 1993*, p. 84.
9. Population Reference Bureau. *1997 world population data sheet*. Washington, DC: Population Reference Bureau, 1997.
10. World Bank, *World development report 1993*, p. 115.
11. Cates, W., T. M. M. Farley, and P. J. Rowe. Worldwide patterns of infertility: Is Africa different? *Lancet* 2(8455):596–98, 1985.
12. Mills, A., J. P. Vaughan, D. L. Smith, and I. Tabibzadeh. *Health system decentralization: Concepts, issues and country experience*. Geneva: WHO, 1990.
13. Pitanguy, J. Feminist politics and reproductive rights: The case of Brazil. In: G. Sen and R. Snow, eds. *Power and decision: The social control of reproduction*. Cambridge: Harvard University Press, 1994.
14. Gomes, C. Strengthening the collaboration between private and public sector for family planning expansion: A case study from Brazil. In: J. Satia, C. Schonmeyr, and S. Tahir, eds. *Managing a new generation of population programmes: Challenges of the nineties*. Kuala Lumpur, Malaysia: International Council on Management of Population Programmes, 1994.
15. Elu, M. del C. Abortion yes, abortion no, in Mexico. *Reproductive Health Matters* 1:58–66, 1993.
16. Lamas, M. The feminist movement and the development of political discourse on voluntary motherhood in Mexico. *Reproductive Health Matters* 10:58–63, 1997.
17. Kolehmainen-Aitken, R.-L., and W. C. Newbrander. *Decentralizing the management of health and family planning programs*. Lessons from FPMD. Boston: Management Sciences for Health, 1997.
18. Plata, M. I., A. C. Gonzalez V, and A. de la Espriella. A policy is not enough: Women's health policy in Colombia. *Reproductive Health Matters* 6:107–13, 1995.
19. Eschen, A. New laws limit access to family planning in Colombia. *AVSC News* 35(2):1, 1997.
20. Bruce, J. *Fundamental elements of the quality of care: A simple framework*. New York: Population Council, 1989.
21. Aitken, I., and L. Reichenbach. Reproductive and sexual health services: Expanding access and enhancing quality. In: G. Sen, A. Germaine,

and L. C. Chen, eds. *Population policies reconsidered.* Cambridge: Harvard University Press, 1994.
22. Fathalla, M. F. The long maternal road to maternal death. *People* 14(3):8–9, 1987.
23. Simmons, R., M. A. Koblinsky, and J. Phillips. Client relations in South Asia: Programmatic and societal determinants. *Studies in Family Planning* 17(6):257–68, 1986.
24. McGirr, N., L. Lacey, C. Woodsong, M. Sherman, and A. G. Johnston. *Decentralization of population and family planning programs: Worldwide experience. Part II: Case studies.* OPTIONS II Project. The Futures Group International, Washington, DC, 1994.
25. Thomason, J. A., and W. C. Newbrander. Health financing and budgeting. In: J. A. Thomason, W. C. Newbrander, and R.-L. Kolehmainen-Aitken, eds. *Decentralization in a developing country: The experience of Papua New Guinea and its health service.* Canberra: Australian National University, National Centre for Development Studies, 1991.
26. Kolehmainen-Aitken, R.-L. The impact of decentralization on health workforce development in Papua New Guinea. *Public Administration and Development* 12:175–91, 1992.
27. World Health Organization. *Mother-baby package: Implementing safe motherhood in countries.* WHO/FHE/MSM/94.11. Geneva: WHO, 1994.
28. World Health Organization. *Integration of health care delivery.* Technical Report Series No. 861. Geneva: WHO, 1996.
29. Aitken, I. W. The health services of Papua New Guinea. In: J. A. Thomason, W. C. Newbrander, and R.-L. Kolehmainen-Aitken, eds. *Decentralization in a developing country: The experience of Papua New Guinea and its health service.* Canberra: Australian National University, National Centre for Development Studies, 1991.
30. Newbrander, W. C., I. W. Aitken, and R.-L. Kolehmainen-Aitken. Performance of the health system under decentralization. In: J. A. Thomason, W. C. Newbrander, and R.-L. Kolehmainen-Aitken, eds. *Decentralization in a developing country: The experience of Papua New Guinea and its health service.* Canberra: Australian National University, National Centre for Development Studies, 1991.
31. Nasah, B. T., and M. Tyndall. Emerging problems of maternity care in urban settings. In: B. T. Nasah, J. K. G. Mati, and J. M. Kasonde, eds. *Contemporary issues in maternal health care in Africa.* Luxembourg: Harwood Academic Publishers, 1994.
32. Lacey, L., C. Woodsong, and N. McGirr. *Decentralization of population and family planning programs: The case of Anglophone Africa.*

Presentation at the annual meeting of the Population Association of America, Miami, FL, 1994.
33. Karim, R. Much good can flow from decentralization. *World Health Forum* 15(2):120–21, 1994.
34. Haines, A. Brazil: Progress in decentralizing health care. *Lancet* 341 (8857):1403, 1993.
35. Bennett, J., J. Ng'weshemi, and T. Boerma. Introduction. In: *HIV prevention and AIDS care in Africa: A district level approach*. Amsterdam: Royal Tropical Institute, 1997.
36. Campos-Outcalt, D., and P. Vickers. For fuller use of health data. *World Health Forum* 9:405–8, 1988.
37. Technical Assistance, Inc., and Management Sciences for Health. *Local initiatives program, Bangladesh*. Final Report 1987–97. Boston: Management Sciences for Health, 1997.
38. Taylor, C. E., and B. B. Berelson. Comprehensive family planning based on maternal/child health services: A feasibility study for a world program. *Studies in Family Planning* 2:22–54, 1971.
39. Simmons, R., and J. Phillips. The integration of family planning with health and development. In: R. L. Lapham and G. B. Simmons, eds. *Organizing for effective family planning programs*. Washington, DC: National Academy Press, 1987.
40. Jenniskens, F., E. Obwaka, S. Kirisuah, et al. Syphilis control in pregnancy: Decentralization of screening facilities to primary care level, a demonstration project in Nairobi, Kenya. *International Journal of Gynecology and Obstetrics* 48 (suppl): S121–28, 1995.
41. Plummer, F. A., et al. Postpartum upper genital tract infections in Nairobi, Kenya: Epidemiology, etiology, and risk factors. *Journal of Infectious Diseases* 156:92–98, 1987.
42. Centers for Disease Control and Prevention. Administration of zidovudine during late pregnancy and delivery to prevent perinatal HIV transmission—Thailand, 1996–1998. *JAMA* 279 (14):1061–62, 1998.
43. Farley, T. M. M., et al. Intrauterine devices and pelvic inflammatory disease: An international perspective. *Lancet* 339:785–88, 1992.
44. Mayaud, P., H. Grosskurth, J. Changalucha, et al. Risk assessment and other screening options for gonorrhea and chlamydial infections in women attending rural Tanzanian antenatal clinics. *Bulletin of the World Health Organization* 73:621–30, 1995.
45. Pacheco, M. E., G. Rodriguez, A. J. Lopez, L. Varela, and N. Murray. *The impact of incorporating educational strategies for AIDS prevention and control into family planning programs*. Final Technical Report. Mexico

City: Fundación Mexicana para la Planificación Familiar and Population Council, 1990.
46. Vernon, R., G. Ojeda, and R. Murad. Incorporating AIDS prevention activities into a family planning organization in Colombia. *Studies in Family Planning* 21 (6):335–43, 1990.
47. Coeytaux, F. *Celebrating mother and child on the fortieth day: The Sfax Tunisia postpartum program.* Quality No. 1. New York: Population Council, 1989.
48. Potter, J. E., O. Mojarro, and L. Nunez. The influence of health care on contraceptive acceptance in rural Mexico. *Studies in Family Planning* 18:144–56, 1987.
49. Chhabra, S., N. Gupta, A. Mehta, and A. Shende. Medical termination of pregnancy and concurrent contraceptive adoption in rural India. *Studies in Family Planning* 19:244–47, 1988.
50. Kay, B. J., and S. M. Kabir. A study of costs and behavioral outcomes of menstrual regulation services in Bangladesh. *Social Science and Medicine* 26:597–604, 1988.
51. Desia, S. Women's burdens: Easing the structural constraints. In: G. Sen, A. Germaine, and L. C. Chen, eds. *Population policies reconsidered.* Cambridge: Harvard University Press, 1994.
52. Walley, J. D., and M. McDonald. Integration of mother and child health services in Ethiopia. *Tropical Doctor* 21:32–35, 1991.
53. Fong, C. O., K. W. Kim, and G. D. Ness. Integration and family planning performance: An interpretive summary. Quoted in Simmons, R., and J. Phillips. The integration of family planning with health and development. In: R. L. Lapham and G. B. Simmons, eds. *Organizing for effective family planning programs.* Washington, DC: National Academy Press, 1987.
54. Pratt, R., S. Acharya, F. Lubis, et al., quoted in K. Hardee and K. Yount. *From rhetoric to reality: Reproductive health promises through integrated services.* Family Health International Working Papers No. WP95-01. Research Triangle Park, NC: Family Health International, 1995.
55. Reilly, Q. Experience of decentralization in Papua New Guinea. In: A. Mills, J. P. Vaughan, D. L. Smith, and I. Tabibzadeh, eds. *Health system decentralization: Concepts, issues and country experience.* Geneva: WHO, 1990.

8

The Impact of Decentralization on Hospitals

William Newbrander

DECENTRALIZATION OF THE HEALTH SECTOR is a prevalent theme in international health policy discussions. Yet decentralization has rarely been discussed in terms of its effects on hospitals, despite their critical role in all health systems. Hospitals are the largest, most visible, and most costly operational units of a country's health system, and they account for a large portion of the health sector's financial, human, and capital resources. In aggregate terms, hospitals in most countries account for nearly half of the total national expenditure for the health sector, consume 50 to 80 percent of recurrent governmental health-sector expenditures, and use a large proportion of the most highly trained health personnel.

This chapter provides a synopsis of how different countries have decentralized their hospital sectors and reviews the key areas where hospitals have been affected by decentralization of the health sector. It also presents a case study of hospital autonomy.

Forms of Decentralized Hospitals

Decentralization involves much more than a simple declaration of "bottom-up" decision making or the reorganization of a government's administrative structure. As governments decentralize their health systems, they are immediately faced with decisions about how resources should be managed and which resources should be managed by local government units and which nationally. Given the large resources that hospitals consume and their high visibility in a nation's health system, these decisions become particularly demanding in the hospital sector. A few examples illustrate the diverse ways that hospitals have been decentralized.

Chile effectively established two discrete systems for hospitals and basic health services in the way it finances and organizes these services. Hospitals and public health services are *deconcentrated* to 27 autonomous health service areas, funded from the National Health Fund. The basic health services, in turn, are *devolved* to 325 municipalities, whose recurrent costs are reimbursed based on a preestablished fee system.

Nicaragua initially *deconcentrated* the management of all hospitals to their respective SILAIS (integrated local health systems). However, this decision was revised fairly quickly. Now the five largest hospitals are each considered the equivalent of a SILAIS in the way they are managed, and they are no longer subordinate to the SILAIS in whose geographic area they are located. The rest of the hospitals continue to be managed by the SILAIS they belong to but maintain a separate budget allocation from the central government.

The Philippines has undergone a far-reaching *devolution* of health services to over 1,600 Local Government Units, ranging from provinces to cities and municipalities. Effective January 1, 1993, nearly all health programs in the Philippines, including 400 of the 440 national government hospitals, were transferred to the 78 provinces and 1,543 municipalities. This transfer included all personnel, facilities, equipment, and other assets of the Department of Health except those specifically designated to remain part of the national government. The Local Government Code totally removed hospital and public health services from central financial and managerial control. By assigning basic outpatient and disease control services to municipalities and hospital services to provinces, the previous integration of these complementary services was destroyed. Furthermore, the new decentralized responsibilities do not correspond to previously developed management capacities.

Papua New Guinea, which has about 15 years' experience with decentralization, initially *decentralized* hospital services to provincial governments through their Assistant Secretaries of Health. The national teaching hospital in the capital city was kept as a national Department of Health responsibility. Within about five years, the second largest hospital was also returned to national control after frequent problems with the provincial government. Hospital budgets are formulated at the provincial level and thus compete with the funding of basic health services and public health activities. Over time, all the other hospitals experienced substantial resource constraints and management problems. This finally led to a policy decision to *recentralize* all hospitals over time, starting with the referral hospitals (base hospitals). Recently, hospital boards were adopted as a new management mode, but it is too early to say how this will affect the decentralization decision.

In Gambia, hospitals have been decentralized by putting them under the authority of hospital boards. They receive budgets from the government and have the authority to spend the money as deemed necessary for the operation of the hospital.

These examples show the choices that countries can make in decentralizing hospitals. Some countries, such as the Philippines, have devolved authority to local governments; others, such as Papua New Guinea, have delegated authority to local governments. Authority over hospital operations has been deconcentrated to lower administrative levels of the health system in Nicaragua, or given to hospital boards that are substantially outside the control of both the health sector and the government in Gambia.

Key Issues

Five main issues arise when evaluating a country's experience in decentralizing the hospital sector:

1. *Role*: integration of hospital services with other health services
2. *Operations*: management of hospitals

3. *Finances*: financing and financial control of hospitals
4. *Human resources*: planning and management of hospital staff
5. *Logistics*: supplies and equipment in hospitals

Role

When hospital services are integrated with other levels and health services within the health system, the roles of hospitals relative to other decentralized units may not be clearly defined. Linkages for coordination, control, and support are rarely explicitly specified, leaving the relationship between hospital management and the management of other complementary health services ambiguous. How could a hospital, its staff, and facilities support rural health staff? What should its role be in in-service training, maintenance of clinical standards, supervision? What should the role of a hospital board be vis-à-vis a district health board in planning health services? Are there special hospital characteristics (size, patient load, type of cases treated, teaching responsibilities) that dictate a larger degree of differentiation in the way hospitals and basic health services are decentralized?

Operations

Some of the key issues for the management of hospitals include control of hospital operations, maintenance of clinical standards, adequacy of managerial capabilities, and development and maintenance of appropriate management information systems.

In some countries, where decentralization has vested powers in local government, politicians have attempted to exert strong local control over the substantial hospital resources. An example is the issuance of noncompetitive contracts for such hospital services as housekeeping, catering, and provision of supplies. To what extent do the decentralization arrangements leave a hospital open to such political influence?

Where decentralization of hospitals has occurred through a collective grouping, such as a hospital board, board of trustees, or board of directors, the effectiveness of such a board in articulating the hospital's mission and values and in protecting its assets is dependent on the autonomy the board has been given to execute its functions and on the commitment and management capacity of the board members. Some countries, such as Ghana, have found that educational programs are necessary to orient and train board members for their new roles.

The managerial relationship between hospitals and basic health services is frequently complicated by the dissimilar levels of qualifications of their managers. Commonly, hospitals are managed by respected, senior clinicians, whereas basic health services are run by more junior public health staff. When hospitals have been made subordinate to local health systems whose top managers are seen as less qualified, problems have occurred.

Decentralization may fracture an existing management information system by severing previous reporting linkages, information flows, and system support for the health facilities. Who should decide what information is to be collected and how the data should flow? How can those responsible for disease control at the national level be assured of up-to-date communicable disease information from autonomous or semiautonomous hospitals? When hospital boards are in charge of budgets that are made up of locally raised revenue and national budget resources, what incentives do the hospitals have to submit such data to national health planners?

Finances

There is an inherent conflict between maintaining high-cost hospital services and expending money to extend and improve primary health services. With financial control delegated or devolved to local authorities, the central health ministry loses any influence it had in protecting certain programs or appropriations. In Papua New Guinea, for instance, negotiations for provincial budgets and staffing were conducted between the individual provinces and the central Departments of Finance and Planning and of Personnel Management. As a result, serious problems were encountered in ensuring adequate budgetary resources for such essential services as transport of hospital doctors on supervisory visits to rural health facilities and maintenance of capital stock. With decentralization there is often a delegation of financial control and revenue-generating capabilities to the local authorities, which may lack the capacity to take on those functions. The case in the Philippines is a dramatic example.

The financial sustainability of hospitals in most countries requires the introduction or expansion of cost-sharing, the retention of a large proportion of fees collected at the local level, and improvements in the management of the hospital and its resources. In Gambia, hospitals have the authority to set their own user charges and retain the revenue collected. In Kenya, fees are set centrally, and 25 percent of the revenue is given to district health authorities. Will the decentralized hospitals have the authority to set their own fee levels and retain the collected revenue? How will the proper financial control of these and other financial resources be ensured? How will increased local decision making and priority setting and the various revenue collection efforts affect the equity of service provision in different regions of the country? Are there any mechanisms to address such national questions after decentralization?

In Kenya, in addition to developing the systems and procedures for collecting and spending funds locally, a local decision-making process was established at the district level, initially to oversee the cost-sharing program. Community-based groups, called District Health Management Boards, were established to oversee the cost-sharing program, which included developing local budgets, developing documents to initiate the spending of these funds, and reviewing district hospitals. On the administrative side, District Health Management Teams were formed to assist in coordination among the health professionals within the district. Links to the local government, particularly the district treasury and district accountant, were established as part of the control procedures for cost-sharing funds.

Since the first district boards were formed five years ago, many boards have performed well and are expected to receive additional responsibilities under the various decentralization options being considered by the Ministry of Health (MOH). Other boards have received mixed or poor reviews. Overall, the experience has provided models for increased decentralization. The systems and procedures for managing cost-sharing funds can become the basis for expanded systems if the current proposals for block grants to selected districts are implemented. Although the cost-sharing program was initiated without having an explicit decentralization policy in place, the program has encouraged and facilitated the promulgation of such a policy in Kenya. The process has been evolutionary, rather than revolutionary, in terms of the speed of change.

Human Resources

Decentralization may result in variations in remuneration and in the terms and conditions of employment of health staff. This, in turn, will affect the distribution of health staff among hospitals and between hospitals and basic health services. It is in the interest of hospitals to stay within budget when staffing vacant slots. In some countries, however, this may result in a scarcity of essential staff for basic health services, either in the same geographic area or elsewhere in the country. What mechanisms are in place to correlate the staffing needs of hospitals and basic health services with the outputs of training programs in the short term and with national human resources planning efforts in the long term? How are national equity concerns being addressed if each hospital is allowed to compete for staff by setting its own salary scales and terms and conditions of service? Is each hospital free to set its own system of staff discipline and performance incentives?

Logistics

Difficulty in procuring drugs and medical supplies is often one of the first problems to be manifested under decentralization. Hospitals have little control over procurement, storage, supply, and transportation of such commodities. In the Philippines, for instance, no provision was made to modify provincial government supply systems after decentralization. As a result, provinces were forced to use their standard pre-decentralization procurement systems, which were not equipped for medical supplies. As a result, provincial hospitals experienced long stockouts of basic supplies and drugs.

The maintenance of health facilities and their equipment is usually transferred to decentralized units, but seldom with the corresponding financial resources and expertise. Local governments are frequently unwilling to budget adequate resources for the repair and maintenance of capital equipment. When medical equipment maintenance is decentralized to the works department of the local government, problems are almost inevitable. Most works departments have little capacity to maintain highly specialized hospital equipment such as x-ray machines, ultrasound scanners, or centrifuges. In Papua New Guinea, this was a frequent cause of frustration for hospital managers.

Hospital Autonomy: A Form of Decentralization

One form of decentralization is hospital autonomy. (1) A public hospital that has moved from being part of the public-sector health system, with all its bureaucratic management constraints, to having a greater degree of freedom in determining how the hospital is governed and managed can be described as autonomous. Faced with difficulties in funding health services, some governments have granted greater autonomy to hospitals to facilitate management improvements, which are expected to lead to improved efficiency in operations, better quality of care, increased revenue generation and financial sustainability, increased public accountability, and expanded choice for consumers. Kenya's conversion of Kenyatta National Hospital (KNH), the government's large national referral and teaching hospital, to a state corporation in 1987 is an example of an experiment with hospital autonomy. The information presented here is current as of 1996, when the study was done.

For some years, KNH had experienced problems with overcrowding; poor quality of care; and shortages of equipment, supplies, and committed, well-trained staff. This was attributed mainly to management weaknesses, both in structure and in staffing; to the absence of good management systems and controls; and to the fact that decision making was centralized in the MOH. With the change to a state corporation, overall ownership of the hospital was retained by the government through the Minister of Health, but a hospital board was delegated responsibility for the assets, liabilities, and development and management of the hospital. The government continued to provide annual development and recurrent funding and retained control over board appointments, funding levels, fee structures, and staff remuneration levels. The board was given the authority to generate revenue through cost-sharing; to procure goods and services, including the hiring and firing of staff; and to use available resources to accomplish the mission of KNH. The specific areas of change are shown in Table 8.1.

Although the new board took legal responsibility and authority in April 1987, a lack of preparation for the change to a state corporation meant that it was some months before the board was operational. Longer delays occurred in strengthening KNH management, due to the reluctance of some managers to accept change and to salary limitations that made it difficult to attract experienced managers from outside the MOH. Thus the hospital continued to be run by the MOH and the hospital director for some time.

With increasing government concern about the slow progress in achieving the desired improvements, a management contract was awarded to a European hospital management firm in late 1991 to speed up the implementation of change. There was considerable internal resistance to the management firm, partly because the board and senior management had been excluded from participating in development of the contract, and partly because of the inexperience of some members of the contracted management team. The contract was rescinded in August 1992. The impact of KNH's becoming an autonomous hospital is reviewed in the following sections.

Operations

Until 1992, the board had little involvement in management, with the hospital director, in conjunction with the MOH, making most of the decisions. In mid-1992, however, a new director was appointed, and he involved the board in the decision-making process. The

Table 8.1 Distribution of Authority Before and After KNH Became a State Corporation

Area	Before State Corporation	After State Corporation
Ownership	Government	Government
Management	MOH	Hospital board composed of civil servants and persons appointed by the government
Hospital policy	MOH	Hospital board
Allocation of government resources to hospital	Treasury and MOH (line-item budget)	Treasury and MOH (block grant)
Allocation of resources within hospital	MOH	Hospital board
Use of cost-sharing revenue	Treasury (excess over budgeted amount)	Hospital board
Setting user fees	MOH	Hospital board with approval of MOH
Hiring and firing staff	MOH	Hospital board
Salary and benefits	Government	Government
Procurement	MOH	Hospital board
Maintenance	Ministry of Works	Hospital board

board, with its blend of experienced private-sector representatives and senior civil servants, began to help with internal issues, such as personnel, and with external issues, such as government funding. A number of management improvements resulted. Senior administrative management was strengthened with the transfer of qualified personnel from other government departments. Clinical management was also improved with greater involvement of medical specialists from the College of Health Sciences, a more clearly defined departmental structure, and more delegation of authority to department heads. KNH specialists were no longer subject to transfer by the MOH, and their salaries were commensurate with those of their public university colleagues.

Evidence of improvements in hospital efficiency due to better management is circumstantial: the overall bed occupancy rate increased slightly but varied considerably among hospital departments, with the pediatrics occupancy rate rising most significantly. The overall average length of stay remained fairly constant after autonomy, although the Medicine Department and Private Wing showed a clear reduction. Productivity may have improved as the overall number of staff declined in relation to the quantity of services provided. Allocation of staff also improved; staffing imbalances were addressed to some degree, with increases in nursing and decreases in subordinate staff.

Staff

Although some staff elected to leave KNH in order to remain MOH employees, the majority elected to become KNH employees and remain at the hospital. Those government staff who elected to become KNH employees retained the right to their government pensions but also joined the new KNH contributory pension scheme in 1991. Later increases in government salary grades meant that KNH could begin to attract nurses away from the private sector, although it still could not compete with the private sector for skilled staff in areas such as computers, finance, and information management. Most of the administrative managers and staff are still from the public sector, in part because even the upgraded government salaries are too low to attract people from the private sector.

Many of the delays in implementing autonomy were a result of the hospital staff's inability to take on more responsible roles. In addition, there was a lack of preparation in the critical management areas to be taken over by KNH, such as planning, personnel, finance and accounting, procurement, and benefits management. This was compounded by the lack of information provided to staff about the changes and the resulting unease about job security, pensions, and pending promotions.

Logistics

The supplies situation improved, primarily due to increased financial resources, speedier payment of bills, freedom to procure directly, and some internal decentralization of supplies management. Nevertheless, problems with slow, inappropriate, and irregular procurement and with internal leakages persisted for quite a while because some staff continued to resist change. Additionally, there was insufficient capacity building among the staff to undertake their new positions, which required handling more sophisticated, computerized logistics systems.

Finances

Expenditures on staff have risen in local currency terms but fallen as a percentage of total recurrent expenses and appear to consume a much smaller share of the total budget than the equivalent figure for the MOH. Operating costs appear to have fallen in real terms, but it is not clear to what degree that is related to increased efficiencies, funding shortages, or other reasons, and financial and service data are not always reliable or consistently collected and reported by KNH.

Government funding to KNH changed to a block grant, which increased budgetary flexibility; this, along with greater control, resulted in more effective internal use of funds. Financial management improvements resulted in more timely, detailed, and accurate financial statements. Financial accountability improved, as demonstrated by a satisfactory audit by a major donor, the US Agency for International Development (USAID). As a state corporation, KNH gained the ability to prosecute staff for fraud, and several people were prosecuted, which served as a deterrent to others. Further improvements, such as computerizing the accounting system and decentralizing financial responsibility, are constrained by the limited ability of existing staff and the difficulty of attracting experienced new staff because of low government pay scales.

KNH's share of MOH development and recurrent funding allocations has risen significantly since it became a state corporation. This may have helped KNH to improve the quality of care but gave rise to concerns about the impact on funding for other MOH services, such as primary and preventive care. The main problem seems to be that the allocation of funds to KNH and to other MOH services is made in somewhat of a vacuum. There is no clear definition of the range, level, and volume of services for each type of facility that could be used as a basis for determining the most cost-effective distribution of resources.

Since it became a state corporation, KNH has been able to retain all its cost-sharing revenue. This has become an important additional source of funding, increasing from 1 percent of KNH's recurrent income in 1986–87 to approximately 10 percent in 1993–94. A wider, more complex, and higher schedule of fees has since been introduced by the board.

Increased autonomy at KNH has improved its ability to negotiate, plan, implement, and be accountable for donor assistance projects and to report on its performance against certain benchmarks. At the same time, the increased managerial flexibility and skills developed as a result of autonomy have helped KNH to appreciate and apply lessons learned under such donor projects. The increased autonomy has also allowed KNH to deal directly with public relations issues; this has enabled the hospital to achieve a more balanced press coverage, with fewer disaster stories and more positive ones being reported.

Role

The role of KNH in the national health care system has been strengthened somewhat by its increased autonomy. Reductions in outpatient attendance and in the size of the hospital freed hospital resources and increased KNH's ability to serve as the national referral hospital. Although a shift of primary health care patients to other facilities in Nairobi was planned, it is not clear whether the reduction in use was a result of decreased utilization by the poor or other vulnerable groups or where those patients actually went for services. Staff believe that the improvements in technical efficiency and quality of care occurred mainly because of the increased availability of supplies, improvements in building and equipment maintenance, and the beneficial impact of those factors on staff productivity. An example is the restoration of respiratory support to the neonatal unit.

Donor assistance has been an important factor in the changes. Agreed-upon conditions placed on grant and loan assistance have encouraged the government and MOH to adhere to funding agreements and the board and management to focus on both long-term structural and system needs and capacity building. In addition, whereas increased autonomy has provided a foundation for management improvement, donor-funded technical assistance has contributed to improvements in system development and capacity. This technical assistance includes early help in developing management options and priorities, the support of management consultants engaged under the World Bank project, and aid with cost-sharing, financial management, efficiency, management, and training provided through USAID's Kenya Health Care Financing Project, which includes the development of KNH's own management training unit.

Lessons Learned

Decentralization of hospitals is often the result of conflict among the national, central, and peripheral levels rather than a carefully planned and rational evolution of a decentralized management system for the health sector. The effects on hospital operations and services provided to the community are less than optimal when decentralization occurs in such an unplanned manner. Some of the key issues that should be anticipated when decentralizing power to hospitals within a health system are as follows.

Capacity Issues

Peripheral or provincial politicians, administrators, and local hospital boards often are not equipped to make complex decisions. For instance, they want the technology and services of the hospital but are unwilling to fund the maintenance necessary for buildings and equipment, the expensive drugs needed, and the salaries to retain clinical staff. Thus, dealing with the complexity of hospitals, staff, operations, and technology requires that politicians, hospital managers, and hospital board members at the peripheral level be educated about the hospital's role, organization, functions, and financing.

The Extent of Decentralization

Many countries may want to reflect on the experiences of others and consider whether hospitals should be decentralized and, if so, to what extent. Some believe that it is politically expedient to decentralize to the district level; others have found that decentralizing only to the regional level is more prudent. The issue of resources is a major concern when considering the appropriate extent of decentralization for hospitals. For hospitals, which are resource-intensive, an intermediate approach of extending decentralization to only the regional level may be the best means of ensuring adequate financing. Financing for hospitals from the national level may be advantageous if it ensures a stable base of resources. The authority to retain fees at the local level is another important element of decentralized hospital administration. The capacity of decentralized hospitals to be effectively managed is another key concern, since lack of adequate capacity may lead to deterioration of the quality of care at a decentralized district hospital. If a decision is made to decentralize hospitals, the administration of these hospitals should rely on a mix of local and national capacities: local-level staff are responsible for day-to-day management, and the more difficult standard setting, monitoring, and supervision are provided by the national level. This mixed decentralized approach ensures support of the referral system as well as improved coordination and supervision of primary health care facilities and services.

Hospital Autonomy

Although many hospitals have derived significant benefits from increased autonomy, a number of steps can be taken to further the goals of improving quality of care, efficiency, revenue generation, and accountability. First, government control may need to be further relaxed to allow a hospital to pursue external funding and to hire better-qualified staff. Second, given the type and level of services provided at hospitals (especially in large referral hospitals) and the difficulty most patients have in paying for these services through fees, the government must ensure that as much of the cost as possible is covered by social insurance, leaving the balance to be covered through targeted government funding. Third, the role of the hospital board remains critical, and the government must maintain a good balance of skilled, experienced private-sector representatives and civil servants and avoid appointments resulting from patronage. Fourth, hospitals need stronger midlevel management capacity and better systems, especially in the areas of finance and supplies, so that efficiency and quality can be maximized. Fifth, hospitals' role in the national system, and their desired type, range, and volume of services and expected client profile, must be defined so that there is a sound basis for determining donor inputs and government capital and recurrent funding levels. Finally, the government should establish and monitor coverage, efficiency, quality of care, and financial performance targets for the hospitals.

These are some of the lessons learned from the challenge of decentralizing power to hospitals. It is anticipated that with increased experiences with decentralization and hospital autonomy, these lessons will be expanded and refined so as to benefit many other countries as they seek to decentralize.

References

1. This section is based on Collins, D., G. Njeru, J. Meme, and W. Newbrander. Hospital autonomy: The experience of Kenyatta National Hospital. Submitted for publication, 1998.

Chapter References

Hume, M., R.-L. Kolehmainen-Aitken, E. Villa, and T. Vian. *Planning and implementing health programs under decentralization: The case of the Philippines.* Paper presented at the 124th meeting of the American Public Health Association. Boston: Management Sciences for Health, 1996.

Kolehmainen-Aitken, R.-L., and W. Newbrander. *Decentralizing the management of health and family planning programs.* Lessons from FPMD series. Boston: Management Sciences for Health, 1997.

Newbrander, W., H. Barnum, and J. Kutzin. Hospital economics and financing in developing countries. WHO Document WHO/SHS/NHP/92.2. Geneva: WHO, 1992.

Thomason, J., W. Newbrander, and R.-L. Kolehmainen-Aitken. *Decentralization in a developing country: The experience of Papua New Guinea and its health service.* Canberra: Australian National University, National Centre for Development Studies, 1991.

PART III
Case Study

Decentralization in Indonesia: An Evolutionary Process

Robert S. Northrup

DECENTRALIZATION IS CURRENTLY an important priority and objective in the Indonesian health system, as evidenced by the nature of recent World Bank–financed loan projects—Health Project IV (HP-IV) and Community Health and Nutrition III (CHN-III)—whose aim is to strengthen the capacity of district health departments to manage their health services effectively. Unlike in a number of other countries, however, the process in Indonesia has been a slow and incremental one, in contrast to the convulsive, nearly overnight conversions driven largely by political forces that have disrupted the health systems in countries such as the Philippines and Zambia.

Arriving in Indonesia to work in 1974, I experienced the centralized system as I taught medical students at Gadjah Mada University how to manage the basic 13 health center programs. In the 1980s I participated as a short-term consultant to the Comprehensive Health Improvement Program—Province Specific (CHIPPS). This US Agency for International Development (USAID)–supported project helped three provinces improve their ability to plan and manage health services based on the collection and analysis of local data to identify and characterize health problems and the monitoring and evaluation of interventions to control those problems. More recently I helped develop the aforementioned HP-IV for the World

Bank, assessed the current status of data gathering and use in districts in two of the project's five provinces, and assisted in the workshops held for district health office staff to strengthen their capacity to collect, analyze, and use local data for problem solving and planning.

This chapter is my own personal perspective on the decentralization process in Indonesia as experienced over the past 24 years, enriched by interviews with some of the USAID staff and consultants involved with CHIPPS (David Calder, Robert Pratt, and Steven Solter), as well as a recent published summary and evaluation of that project. (1) I subtitled the paper "An Evolutionary Process" to emphasize the incremental nature of the decentralization process as well as its slowness, but other subtitles would have been appropriate as well: "The Reluctant Suitor," to emphasize what seemed to be the central ministry's hesitancy to commit itself to decentralization; "Slow but Sure?" to note the possibility that the center may never be willing to let go of the reins; or "The Chicken or the Egg?" to raise the question whether changing the capacity and activities of peripheral staff, as in CHIPPS, led to decentralization or whether decentralization led to changed staff activities and capacity. Each of the subtitles captures an important aspect of the process.

I review certain aspects of the centralized system as it functioned in the 1970s, describe CHIPPS and its accomplishments, characterize HP-IV as one formal step toward decentralization, and then draw conclusions about lessons learned from this process that might be of use in other countries on the road to decentralization.

1970s: A Highly Centralized System

As seen from the field level in the 1970s, Indonesia's government health system was almost entirely centrally planned and managed. Health center staff carried out some dozen basic activities, ranging from direct patient care to school health, immunization, water and sanitation, and malaria control. Many of these areas were run as vertical programs from a central ministry technical and management unit down to a dedicated field-worker, with immunization and family planning being the most visible examples of such vertical nonintegrated structures. Certainly integration was not a high priority at that time.

Implementation directives and targets were set centrally by the divisions (directorates general), subdivisions (directorates), and subdirectorates within the Ministry of Health (MOH) that ran these various programs. Data consisting of reports of activities, although they passed through the district and provincial offices, were collected and analyzed largely by these central units. These reports were compared with centrally set targets based on demographic data that were passed back to the periphery, setting the number of children to be immunized or the number of eligible couples to be convinced about family planning, for example. Certainly there was no objection to local analysis and use of data, but there was little expectation of such use. In those years, graduates from medical schools had little or no preparation in how to move through the sequence of problem definition, solution generation, implementation, monitoring, evaluation, and replanning. Hence it was unusual to find a district that aggressively managed its activities based on the data being collected. Health centers that at least prepared graphs showing progress over months and years and posted them on the health center walls were unique and were recognized with special awards for excellence. Locally based planning and resource allocation were almost absent, which is to say that there was little or no variation in the activities carried out from locality to locality, despite the substantial variation in problems, environment, and local resources among the country's 27 provinces.

The structure at both the provincial and district levels nominally provided (and provides currently) for local decision making. At the provincial level there was both a local office of the MOH responsible for technical direction, planning, and standard setting (Kanwil) and a branch of the provincial government (Dinas) responsible for the implementation of programs. At the district level the head health official was in fact on the staff of the local district government. Yet during this period the heads of the Kanwil and the Dinas at the provincial level were usually the same person, and the district health officers I encountered in the 1970s seemed more directed by MOH directives than by the district government head. Bossert notes that the provincial and district government officials were themselves under the separate vertical authority of the Ministry of Internal Affairs and thus were centrally directed. (1)

Funds collected from health centers and hospitals were passed on to district or provincial nonhealth government units. Because these funds were said to be almost the only flexible funds available to district officials, they were rarely returned to the facilities that collected them. Thus there was little budgetary support for any locally planned efforts beyond the national programs, and health facilities often had no money to pay for simple physical repairs or minor supply or equipment needs. Funds were allocated on the basis of formulas determined by the planning unit within the central ministry, generally on a simple per capita basis, and applied uniformly across the country. This led to some inappropriate allocations. For example, Nusa Tenggara Timur, a largely Christian province, received the same per capita allotment of funds for the provision of medical services to persons going on pilgrimages to Mecca as did provinces that were predominantly Muslim.

Mechanisms for obtaining support for locally determined needs were present. The planning and budgeting process included (and includes) annual submission of a list of local activities and other proposed expenditures (DUP/DIP) and requests for special funds for construction (INPRES). But these mechanisms were often used to request funds for projects determined from above, not those generated from data-based analysis of local health problems or special local health system needs. Human resources were handled similarly. Doctors and some other staff were centrally hired, and their postings were administered centrally, largely on the basis of the aforementioned planning unit formulas rather than in response to local needs. And supervision was often carried out for single programs—for example, for the diarrhea program alone—rather than as a tool for improving the local management of activities or conditions deemed important locally.

1980s: CHIPPS

USAID initiated CHIPPS in the early 1980s with the intention of making health development efforts much more locally determined—province specific. In so doing, USAID was explicitly countering the strong centrally oriented pressures in the MOH. One actor in the effort commented, "The government did not allow use of the word 'decentralization.' They assumed everything was the same everywhere." It was only through the identification of a few "friends" in the planning section of the MOH that the project was able to move forward.

In deciding where to locate the project, USAID explicitly chose provinces that had a history of resenting central authority for various reasons: Aceh, Nusa Tenggara Timur, and West Sumatra. This supported the efforts of the project to use local data to make programs province specific, thus challenging the central government wisdom regarding program balance and strategies as expressed in the standard allocation formulas for resources and programs. The goal was bidirectional—aiming centrally to empower provinces to negotiate more effectively for their specific needs with the center, and aiming peripherally to improve management and operational planning by stimulating local responses to local needs based on local data.

The project provided, at the provincial level, technical assistance in the form of a resident epidemiologist or health planner, funds to support the collection and analysis of data such as surveys, and funds to support actions determined on the basis of the local data analysis. It also supported workshops and seminars among CHIPPS participants to allow the sharing of methods, findings, and solutions to problems. These gatherings of participants were particularly important in building sufficient self-esteem and confidence to maintain momentum against continuing resistance from the center.

The local data surprised the central planners, showing that the current system was not working. Studies demonstrated a high incidence of neonatal tetanus, accompanied by a coverage rate for completed tetanus immunizations among pregnant women of only 3 to 4 percent, much lower than had been expected. This led to a significant change in policy, from one of seeking to administer two tetanus immunizations during pregnancy to one of seeking to immunize all women of childbearing age.

The CHIPPS studies demonstrated that the tuberculosis case-finding strategies were picking up only a small proportion of the active cases. Further exploration defined risk factors for tuberculosis. These were used to formulate guidelines for case finding based on seeking out high-risk populations and individuals, which was more likely to succeed.

The training policy in place at the time was generic, that is, training was given to classes of workers regardless of their need for it. Based on CHIPPS data, the policy was shifted to one based on identification of a behavioral problem, clear definition of the behaviors needed, and development of targeted training to respond to that need.

CHIPPS did a number of studies in the area of inappropriate drug prescribing, demonstrating the high prevalence of polypharmacy and incorrect prescribing and documenting the high cost of these behaviors. This led to a variety of efforts to reduce this wastage and the costs related to it.

In West Sumatra specifically, the CHIPPS efforts moved downward from the provincial level to the *puskesmas* (health center), focusing on the gathering, analysis, and use of data for management at that much more peripheral level. Training, supervision, and other activities were organized to facilitate this more expansive level of decentralized decision making.

In both West Sumatra and Aceh, it was determined that inadequate preparation of health staff during their preservice education was a significant problem, impeding appropriate organization and delivery of services. This led to CHIPPS-supported efforts in both those provinces to develop improved medical school and nursing curricula aimed at preparing undergraduate students to function more effectively in community settings and health centers.

The project's concern for the sustainability of its activities led to proposals to the center, as part of annual budget submissions, to obtain funds to carry out the kind of diagnostic studies CHIPPS was supporting. Since planning activities had been largely top-down, there was no category in the DUP menu of items for problem diagnosis and assessment studies. Because of CHIPPS-related requests, a new DUP category was created for that purpose.

Perhaps the most basic indicator of the project's success was the number of proposals made annually to change the normal DUP/DIP allocations based on provincial and more local data. At its peak, when provincial staff had been adequately prepared for this challenge, three to four such proposals were presented annually. Observers also described a reduction in the feeling of elitism at the center as well, although this is certainly not an objective measure.

From a longer-term perspective, the CHIPPS experience may be seen as providing the critical base of experience in decentralized planning and management that led to the current series of World Bank–funded health projects, most recently HP-IV, aimed specifically at decentralization. It appeared to lead to a gradual recognition by central leaders of the benefits and even the inevitability of some degree of decentralization.

1994: Active Decentralization with HP-IV

With HP-IV, the center's commitment to decentralization is clear, and a variety of project components explicitly support that commitment. Whereas CHIPPS aimed for increasingly independent provincial decision making, HP-IV (and its predecessor HP-III) is directed toward district (*kabupaten*)-level planning and management, with a clear expectation of effective analysis and use of data at the even more peripheral *puskesmas* (health center) level. (*Kabupatens* typically serve 1 to 3 million people, and *puskesmas* serve 10,000 to 30,000. Now in Project Year 3, HP-IV has had an observable impact on district level planning and management, but the old pattern of waiting for direction from above has not completely disappeared.

HP-IV is directed at five provinces representing a mixture of conditions: East Java on the most populated island of Java, with headquarters in Surabaya, Indonesia's second largest and most sophisticated city; Nusa Tenggara Barat on the islands east of Bali, and West Sumatra, both of which are areas of moderate population and sophistication; and East and West Kalimantan, both of which have isolated areas of low population density and minimal infrastructure. The full range of challenges to service delivery is thus represented.

The aim of HP-IV is to bring about measurable improvements in the performance of the health services. The specific deficiencies targeted by the project include underutilization of health services, reflected in low coverage figures for critical services (antenatal care, for example); poor quality of services relative to defined standards of care; inadequate access by the poor and remote; and inefficient and inequitable resource use.

The mechanisms by which these deficiencies are being addressed through the project include:

- At the health facility level, changes through quality assurance activities to bring about increased responsiveness to client needs through improved analytical and problem-solving efforts.
- At the district and provincial levels, decentralization, characterized as planning and active management based on data, to reduce the rigidities and inefficiencies associated with centralized direction and resource allocation.
- Improved mobilization of resources from both local and central/provincial levels.
- Attention to the private sector as a recognized component of health services that must be included in efforts to improve performance.

In addition to hearsay information, access to documents, and observation of planning activities by district teams at national planning sessions, I had the opportunity early in the project to visit 5 of the first 11 districts to receive project inputs and guidance. From these observations and other evidence, it was clear that districts' capacities to carry out the activities and responsibilities envisioned by the project varied extensively.

Some districts, and even some *puskesmas*, had designed and carried out surveys, analyzed the results, and based problem-solving activities on them. Others had one or two staff members who had participated in surveys organized by provincial or central levels but had not conceived of or developed such data-gathering efforts on their own. Others had no experience with this fundamental technique.

Although provinces invariably had numerous staff members with master's degrees in public health, presumably accompanied by skills in data gathering and use of data in planning, districts often had only one or two persons with that level of education, frequently the district health officer himself. Such officers were often caught up in a frenzy of bureaucratic tasks and found it difficult to devote the time needed to identify problems from lengthy lists of figures in reports or to develop prospective data-gathering activities such as surveys to clarify the nature of such problems or diagnose their causes.

Data were abundant. Each program produced a flood of monthly data that was assembled and passed on to the provincial level. But the level of computerization varied, with some districts having no computers at all. Thus staff members' time was occupied by tedious transfer and hand calculating of the data, making further manipulation and analysis of the data to bring out failures to achieve coverage or utilization targets difficult.

The immunization program was a clear exception to these generalities. Part of routine practice at the district level was the activity of "local area monitoring." From the routinely reported numbers of injections given, reports were produced that identified units with activity or coverage failures relative to targets. This automatic analysis made use of the data to bring about corrective action. Certainly immunization is unique in having an effective response to shortfalls in coverage—sending out the troops to find the unimmunized—that can be implemented with only an administrative decision. Such is not the case with diarrhea, in contrast; mothers cannot be commanded to bring their sick children to the clinic for care, and even targets cannot be easily set and will vary from month to month. Yet it was clear that the built-in analytical process used by the immunization program made a significant difference in the use of the data to manage services so that performance targets were reached.

Since initiation of the project, introductory training workshops conducted for successive batches of district teams (11 districts in the first batch, 15 in the second) have introduced new performance indicators and defined analytical processes such as those used by the immunization program to identify service performance problems. The workshops have reviewed the typical cycle of problem identification and solution and have provided practice in brainstorming to generate possible causes of problems and in planning actions to overcome them and their causes. The most recent workshop—round two for the first batch of districts—stressed the need to go beyond brainstorming as the only "diagnostic" activity, the pattern of reaction in the recent past. Districts were encouraged to carry out active data gathering through rapid surveys or focus group discussions in addition to more detailed analyses of existing data. These steps would provide more objective evidence of the causes of problems identified by the initial data analysis, so that corrective actions could be based on more accurate diagnoses of causes and thereby be more cost-effective.

In this second round, there was also a genuine recognition of the importance of private providers and the need to document the quantitative dimensions of their role and improve the quality and effectiveness of services being provided. Based on experience using methods to assess and improve private provider case management practices developed by Basic Support for Institutionalizing Child Survival (BASICS) and tested in India and in Central Java, Indonesia, (2) 11 districts are launching pilot efforts to document and improve private services. This private-sector effort is organized and directed at the level of the district and *puskesmas*, although it uses standard methods for both assessment and intervention efforts.

One senses that, relative to decentralized planning and management, a revolution in action or even in thinking has not yet taken place. The extra funds made available to health centers and districts to support locally determined responses to problems have often been used to support increased numbers of supervisory or community visits, not to respond to specific problems identified proactively from local data. Budgetary process changes have only recently provided true block grants to the district level, and at the recent workshop, most district staff members were unfamiliar or seemingly uncomfortable with methods that set allocation levels on the basis of specific program or location needs or problems, rather than uniformly by simpler criteria such as population. On the central side, specific programs have been reluctant to give up control of how funds are expended and, until this most recent shift to block grants, have requested that peripheral budgets specify a range of action categories for their programs. Districts have been overwhelmed by the demands of preparing such detailed budgets; lacking the logistical capacity to do so, they have retreated to standard formulas based on the action categories. The result has been central control through the budget, despite the appearance of decentralized management. The reaction at the district level seems to have been, Why should we push to have our desires met when the higher-ups have already decided what they will let us have? With the new shift to a true block grant, this residual central planning mechanism has been dissipated, and the potential to achieve real decentralization of decision making has been substantially increased. As new batches of districts proceed through the training and action sequence of the project, we will be able to observe whether acceptance of responsibility for problem identification and solution at the district level, combined with proactive data gathering and attention to the private sector, will actually take place.

Conclusions

Over my 24 years of intermittent observation, a clear but gradual shift has occurred in Indonesia, from a strongly centralized system to one that is on the brink of true decentralization, at least in a few provinces. During the 1970s, although mechanisms that could have allowed peripheral priorities to emerge were present (the DUP/DIP and INPRES budgetary mechanisms, as well as the five-year planning process), both the strong vertical program structure and the commanding central planning unit ensured that decisions and resource allocations were determined from above, often in a uniform manner inconsistent with variation in conditions across the country. CHIPPS began a process of capacity development at the provincial level, showing how data gathering at lower levels could more effectively identify both health and service problems, define the causes and appropriate responses to correct them, and demonstrate when solution had taken place. Pressures on the central level based on such data might well have been the beginning of the more rapid evolution toward decentralization. This accelerating process was fortified by a continuing influx of staff to the provincial and district levels who had had formal public health training and were capable of using data effectively and leading such decentralized planning and management processes. The result can be seen in the current HP-IV, in which the skills needed for data-based assessment of performance and response to identified deficiencies are being explicitly transferred to the district and even *puskesmas* levels. The major change in government funding methods, with the shift to a block grant approach, signifies how far this process has advanced during this relatively short time.

So the process has moved forward, and decentralization is indeed taking place. One might ask at this point, what made it happen? Donors appear to have had some influence on the process. Certainly USAID deserves credit for supporting early activities that demonstrated the importance of data and allowed both the center and the periphery to learn new roles and responsibilities. The World Bank has been a major influence in recent years, as evidenced by the characteristics of the health projects it has funded and the government support of them.

The center has actively supported the shift to decentralized decision making. Initially, most of the support came from the planning unit at the center, but specific programs are now being pulled along as their last budgetary hooks on the periphery have been eliminated. The primary control mechanism now available to the center seems to be the setting of programmatic targets for the periphery and its ability to respond—at least verbally, if not by the issuance of strict commands—to reports on the achievement of those targets. With increased access to good data, even the targets can be challenged by the periphery when they are found to be inconsistent with reality.

Unlike in Zambia and other countries, there has not been a strong political push from the periphery demanding that the center hand over control. This may have helped the decentralization process by allowing it to proceed slowly and incrementally, with gradual acquisition of skills and capacity at the provincial and district levels and gradual letting go of the various mechanisms of control by the central planning and program units.

Certainly there are numerous aspects of planning and management, numerous processes, experiments, and other experiences, that I have skipped over. Yet one might reasonably conclude on the basis of this admittedly superficial and personal review that developing the bottom—peripheral capacity development; pilot efforts in improved data collection, analysis, and use; and gradual accretion of experience at both ends of the top-bottom spectrum—is the approach most likely to result in successful decentralization without a chaotic transition period. Donors can help in this process by supporting contributory activities at the periphery and the center and by not pushing for rapid change. Persistence is a necessary ingredient to ensure that the slow evolutionary process toward decentralization goes forward while avoiding the uproar of rapid change. Finally, the Indonesian experience is convincing evidence that more than the usual donor-funded five-year project length is necessary when effective and responsible decentralization is the goal.

References

1. Bossert, T., R. Soebekti, and N. Kumara Rai. "Bottom-up" planning in Indonesia: Decentralization in the Ministry of Health. *Health Policy and Planning* 6(1):55–63, 1991.
2. Chakraborty, S., A. D'Souza, and R. S. Northrup. Improving private practitioner care of sick children: New approaches tested in rural Bihar, India. Submitted for publication, 1998.

About the Contributors

Riitta-Liisa Kolehmainen-Aitken has 20 years of experience in health system decentralization, health policy formulation, and health planning in developing countries. She has long-term living and working experience in Sierra Leone and Papua New Guinea, and has worked in some 20 countries as a short-term consultant to various donors, including the US Agency for International Development, World Bank, Asian Development Bank, and World Health Organization. In Papua New Guinea, she worked from 1984 to 1989 at the national Department of Health, leading the planning unit that was responsible for formulating national health policy and for producing the country's second five-year health plan. Dr. Kolehmainen-Aitken currently serves as a Senior Program Associate for the MSH-managed Family Planning Management Development project. She has responsibilities in the areas of decentralization, health services and human resources planning, and evaluation. She regularly teaches on decentralization in courses at Boston University School of Public Health and Harvard School of Public Health. She is coeditor/coauthor of two other books on decentralization—*Decentralization in a Developing Country: The Experience of Papua New Guinea and Its Health Service* and *Lessons from FPMD: Decentralizing the Management of Health and Family Planning Programs*—and has published on human resources planning and health systems management. She earned her MD degree from the University of Helsinki and her MPH and DrPH in Health Services Administration from the Harvard School of Public Health.

Iain W. Aitken is a lecturer on Maternal and Child Health and International Health at the Harvard School of Public Health. He has worked for 25 years in health services development in developing countries, including 15 years resident in Papua New Guinea and Sierra Leone. His work in reproductive health started with research and program development in maternal and perinatal health care in those countries, and he has participated in several World Health Organization technical working groups on safe motherhood. He has been involved in the management of decentralized health systems in Papua New Guinea and Africa, and helped to develop a graduate program in Community Health at the University of Papua New Guinea to train health administrators for the decentralized provincial governments there. Recently he has been evaluating the impact of a new maternal and child health financing program within the decentralized health system in Bolivia. He is also researching the determinants of women's preferences for contraceptive technologies. Dr. Aitken earned a medical degree from the University of Cambridge and graduate degrees in Tropical Medicine from the London School of Hygiene and Tropical Medicine and in Public Health (MPH) from Harvard University.

Malcolm Bryant has over 15 years of experience in the management of international health care projects. As Director of MSH's Strengthening Health Services Program, Dr. Bryant provides technical direction to and oversees the management of several health and family planning projects funded by the US Agency for International Development in developing countries. Before coming to MSH in 1995, Dr. Bryant worked as a Clinical Lecturer in Community Health and Epidemiology for the University of Saskatchewan, Canada. Dr. Bryant also served as a Medical Health Officer and Regional Director in the province of Saskatchewan. In this position, he led a multidisciplinary team of 80 health professionals in providing and promoting preventive health care services to a population of 160,000. Until 1991, he held an appointment at the Harvard Institute for International Development (HIID) as a Research Associate and served as a Lecturer in Population Sciences at the Harvard School of Public Health. Before joining HIID, Dr. Bryant spent five years working with the Ministry of Health in Zimbabwe to redesign the national health policy and increase planning capacity at the district and regional levels. Dr. Bryant received his MPH from the Harvard School of Public Health and his medical degree from London Hospital Medical College.

Richard Laing is an Associate Professor in the Department of International Health at Boston University School of Public Health, where he teaches courses on Health Systems Research, Maternal and Child Health, Human Resources Management, Infectious Diseases, and Promoting Rational Drug Use. He previously served as a Senior Program Associate of the Drug Management Program of MSH, working with drug use, the International Network for the Rational Use of Drugs, and the Management Training Program from 1989 to 1995. Dr. Laing also served with the Zimbabwe Ministry of Health as Director of Health Manpower Training, Essential Drugs Training Coordinator, and Provincial Medical Director.

Originally trained as a doctor in Zimbabwe, Dr. Laing undertook postgraduate studies in London and at the Institute for Development Studies in Sussex, England. His major research and consulting activities concern quality of care. In the Philippines, Dr. Laing works on quality assurance in a women's health and safe motherhood project; in Zimbabwe, on the establishment of hospital drug and therapeutic committees in government, mission, and private hospitals. Both countries are at different stages in the decentralization of health services. Dr. Laing is a frequent consultant for the World Health Organization.

Florante P. Magboo is MSH's National Program Monitoring Advisor working in the Office for Public Health Service of the Department of Health (DOH), Manila, the Philippines. In this role, he assesses data needs and assists in developing management information systems for family planning, maternal/child health, and nutrition. He also conducts research and develops tools for monitoring program performance. His previous positions included Rural Health Physician, Fellow of the Field Epidemiology Training Program (FETP), and Medical Specialist for FETP, all with the DOH. Dr. Magboo received his MD degree from the Perpetual Help College of Medicine in Laguna, the Philippines.

William Newbrander, the Director of MSH's Health Reform and Financing Program, is a health economist with 17 years of experience in health financing and hospital administration. He joined MSH in 1992 after having served with the World Health Organization for 8 years in Papua New Guinea, Thailand, and Switzerland. In addition to managing the program, he provides technical assistance for MSH in health reform, national health insurance, hospital management, and decentralization. Dr. Newbrander regularly teaches health financing at MSH, Boston University School of Public Health, the World Bank, and other organizations. He recently directed an international team of experts who studied health sector reform in six Asian countries. That work was the focus of the Asian Development Bank's Second Regional Conference on Health Sector Reform: Issues Related to Private Sector Growth. His publications include a book based on the conference, *Private Health Sector Growth in Asia: Issues and Implications* and a monograph on decentralization coauthored with Riitta-Liisa Kolehmainen-Aitken. He also coauthored *Modelling in Health Care Finance: A Compendium of Quantitative Technique for Health Care Financing*, which is forthcoming from the International Labour Organisation. He holds master's degrees in Hospital Administration and in Economics as well as a PhD in Health Economics from the University of Michigan.

Robert S. Northrup has worked in the area of child health for more than 30 years and has been a consultant for the Rockefeller Foundation, UNICEF, the US Agency for International Development (USAID), and the World Health Organization, among others. He has been a resident advisor in Indonesia, Bangladesh, and Japan and provided technical leadership to the governments of Bangladesh, Haiti, Indonesia, Pakistan, Senegal, Nigeria, Russia, and other countries in areas such as the control of diarrheal disease, development of public-private partnerships to improve the delivery of child health services, vitamin A programs, curriculum development for medical education, local production of vaccines, and development of nutrition programs. For the past 5 years, Dr. Northrup has served as MSH's Senior Technical Officer and Director of the Private Sector Working Group for the worldwide Basics for Institutionalizing Child Survival (BASICS) project, which is funded by USAID and based in Washington, DC. He was previously the Technical Director of the Technologies in Primary Health Care (PRITECH) Project, which focused on worldwide diarrhea control. He assumed this position after 6 years as Chairman of the Department of Community Medicine at the University of Alabama, and was subsequently Professor of Community Health and Director of Primary Care at Brown University Medical School. Dr. Northrup is currently adjunct Professor of International Health at Johns Hopkins School of Public Health and School for Advanced International Studies. His career also includes key administrative and research positions with the Food and Drug Administration and National Institute of Allergy and Infectious Disease in the US. He earned his MD degree from Harvard University.

Jose R. Rodriguez serves as Chief of Party for an MSH team assisting a family planning and child survival project funded by the US Agency for International Development in the Philippines. In this role, he works to strengthen the capacity of provinces and municipalities to manage their programs in the recently decentralized Philippine health system. He has 18 years of experience working in various positions in the Department of Health, including Regional Director of Health. He has served as a trainer for the World Health Organization in Indonesia and Guatemala. Dr. Rodriguez earned his MD degree from the Cebu Institute of Medicine in the Philippines.

Steven Solter is a Principal Program Associate in the Strengthening Health Services program at MSH. He has 26 years of experience in technical areas that include decentralized delivery of health services, district-level management, rural health services, integrated family planning and child survival interventions, safe motherhood initiatives, and epidemiology-based planning. He currently directs MSH's project in the Philippines, which works to strengthen the capability of health officials to manage child survival and family planning programs.

Dr. Solter previously served as a Senior Program Officer in the Technical Unit of MSH's Family Planning Management Development (FPMD) project, where his principal responsibilities were developing tools for family planning and reproductive health programs and providing technical assistance to countries in Africa and Asia. Dr. Solter has also been a long-term resident advisor working with the US Agency for International Development for programs in Afghanistan (1976-79), Indonesia (1980-87), and the Philippines (1990-94). He served as Chief of Party of the Philippines Child Survival Project from 1990 to 1993. Dr. Solter earned an MPH degree from Johns Hopkins University and an MD degree from Stanford University.

Charles C. Stover, a health financing and policy expert and health care administrator, is a Principal Program Associate at MSH, where he specializes in health insurance and managed care systems in developing countries. He has 25 years of experience in international and domestic settings in the government, private, and nonprofit sectors. He recently served as team leader for the Strengthening Health Insurance Project in Mongolia and directed the development of several managed care initiatives in Kenya. From 1992 to 1994, Mr. Stover was Chief of Party of the Health Finance Development Project funded by the US Agency for International Development in the Philippines. He later served as the project's director from Boston, with an all-Filipino team in Manila.

Before joining MSH, Mr. Stover was Executive Director of an HMO, Director of Development of a managed care company, and Chief Operating Officer of a community hospital outside of Boston. He has also served in health- and finance-related posts in government: Commissioner of the Rate Setting Commission, Assistant Secretary of the Executive Office of Human Services, and Interim Director of the State Health Planning Office in Massachusetts. Mr. Stover holds a master's degree in Economics from Princeton University.

Robert J. Timmons, a Senior Fellow at MSH, has applied his extensive experience in designing systems for monitoring and evaluation and in using information for management to a wide variety of health development initiatives in Africa, Asia, Latin America, and the Middle East. His recent activities include assisting the Government of Oman to build a national clinical and management information system for maternal/ child health and birth-spacing programs. His current work in the Philippines continues the work he started in his role as Director of the Management Information Systems (MIS) Program at MSH, where he was responsible for developing management systems for health and family planning programs. Dr. Timmons also spent two years in Turkey as Regional Director of Technical Services for Pathfinder International.

In previous work for MSH, Dr. Timmons assisted the Nigerian Federal Ministry of Health and Family Health Services Project to develop a family planning MIS. Before that, he served as a Research Scientist with Community Systems Foundation in Ann Arbor, Michigan. Dr. Timmons earned a PhD in Urban and Regional Planning, an MS in Biometrics, and an MSW in Policy and Planning from the University of Michigan.

Index

abortions, 112–13, 118
　family planning, 127
　Mexico, 117
　mortality rates, 114
academic institutions. *See* educational institutions
accessibility of services, 12, 34, 117–18, 127–28, 164
accreditation, 75, 90–91, 107
acquired immune deficiency syndrome (AIDS), 113, 124
administrative aspects. *See* management; managers
Africa, 112, 123–24
AIDS. *See* acquired immune deficiency syndrome (AIDS)
Aitken, Iain, 6–7, 132–33n6; 133–34n21; 134nn29, 30; 171–72
American Public Health Association meeting, 2
Aquino, Corazon, 102
Asia, 112
authority. *See* control

Bangladesh, 125–29
barangays. *See* cluster surveys
Basic Support for Institutionalizing Child Survival (BASICS), 166, 184
block grants, 166, 168
boards of directors
　hospitals, 140–41, 150–52
　Kenya, 33, 35
　Kenyatta National Hospital, 144–45
Bolivia, 119, 121, 123–24
Boston University School of Public Health, 2
Brazil, 116–17, 124, 130
Bryant, Malcolm, 3, 172
budgeting
　hospitals, 139
　human resources, 39

Indonesia, 167–168
Kenya, 33
management information systems, 125
provincial/regional levels, 124–25

Cairo. *See* International Conference on Population and Development
Calder, David, 158
Campos-Outcalt, Doug, 55
career development, 58
Cause and Effect in Decentralization, 28*fig*
central/national levels
　control, 15, 18–19
　data collection, 74, 84–85
　family planning programs, 129–31
　hospitals, 151–52
　human resources, 52–54
　Indonesia, 158–61, 166–68
　information needs, 78–79
　long-range goals, 20
　national campaigns, 15
　new roles, 105–6
　pharmaceutical management, 67–71, 100, 121
　Philippines, 29–30, 75
　planners, 20
　resistance to change, 29–30
　roles, 20–21, 59
　staffing, 58
　strategic planning, 20
　surveys, 84–85
　training, 54
certification programs, 90–91, 107
childhood disease, 2, 112
Chile, 115, 138
CHIPPS. *See* Comprehensive Health Improvement Project—Province Specific
CHN-III. *See* Community Health and Nutrition III

civil service, 39–40, 44, 46, 51–52
clients
　hospitals, 151–52
　planning, 14
　privacy, 127
　quality of care, 97
　reproductive health, 118
cluster surveys, 81–85
　design, 82–84
　implementation, 83–84
　sustainability, 92
　training interviewers, 84
　vs. national surveys, 84–85
Colombia, 117, 127
commodities distribution, 80
communication, 21, 24
　organizational structures, 48–50
　planning, 17
　quality of care, 101
　vertical integration, 122
Community Health and Nutrition III (CHN-III), 157
community participation, 21, 24, 125–26
community services, 122–23
Comprehensive Health Improvement Project—Province Specific (CHIPPS), 8, 157–58, 161–63, 167–68
computerization, 165
conflict-resolution mechanisms, 48
contraception
　Colombia, 117
　cost-effective procurement, 121
　maternal mortality, 114
　Philippines, 74–76, 79–80, 84–87, 87*table*
　Social Marketing Project, 76
　vertical integration, 122–23

175

control, 21, 54
  central/national vs. local, 13, 18–19, 41, 47–48
  See also organizational structures
convenience, 12, 34, 117–18, 127–28, 164
coordination, 20, 78
  hospitals, 140
  human resources, 50–53
  planning process, 14
  See also organizational structures
cost-effectiveness, 79
  data collection, 92
  drug procurement, 67
  Kenyatta National Hospital, 148–49
  monitoring strategies, 77–78
  national surveys, 79–80
  pharmaceutical management, 66
  planning process, 13
  reproductive health, 121
cost-sharing, 142–43
  Kenya, 27–28, 31–36, 32*fig*, 146*table*
  Kenyatta National Hospital, 149
  See also cost-effectiveness; financial aspects
cultural issues, 123

data collection, 5, 23–24, 61, 79, 81
  analysis, 165
  central/national levels, 74, 78–80
  cluster surveys, 81–85
  commodities distribution and logistics MIS, 80
  community, 74
  comparison of methods, 79–80
  Family Planning Management Development project, 91, 94–95n9
  focus groups, 166
  health facility assessments, 81
  hospitals, 141
  human resources, 59–60
  identifying at-risk groups, 81
  Indonesia, 157–59, 161–62, 168
  integrated, 73

local levels, 74, 163–64
national surveys, 79–80
provincial/regional levels, 74
quality of care, 81
rapid surveys, 166
sampling, 82–83
staff, 58
survey design, 82–83
sustainability, 92
See also management information systems
decentralization, 11*def*, 16*def*, 40*def*, 65*def*
  advantages, 115
  Cause and Effect in Decentralization, 28*fig*
  common problems, 12–13
  mixed, 151
  obstacles, 15
deconcentration, 65*def*
delegation, 65*def*
democratization of health care, 107, 115
demographic studies, 20, 23
demonstrations by health workers, 103–4
devolution, 65*def*
  human resources, 40
  Philippines, 27–31, 36
Devolution in the Philippines, 29*fig*, 75*table*
disease control, 141
distance learning, 99
Distribution of Authority Before and After KNH Became a State Corporation, 146*table*
district levels
  family planning, 130
  Health Project IV, 163–67
  hospitals, 151
  Indonesia, 157–59, 166–67
  Kenya, 27–28, 33
  doctors, 50, 55, 146
  See also health care workers
donors, 20–21, 49, 54, 98–99, 124
five-year projects, 169
hospitals, 151–52
Indonesia, 168–69
information management, 78, 83
Kenyatta National Hospital, 148, 150
Philippines, 85

See also US Agency for International Development; World Health Organization
drugs
  appropriateness of use, 69, 97, 162
  cost-effective, 66
  essential drug lists (EDL), 66, 70, 121
  generic, 66
  procurement, 3–4, 30–31, 33, 143–44
  public education, 71
  quality of care, 97
  standard treatment guidelines, 68, 70
  storage, 70
  See also pharmaceutical management

economic aspects, 31–32, 40
  See also financial aspects
education, 78, 113
  contraception, 114
  hospital autonomy, 150–51
  Kenya, 32–33
  pharmaceutical management, 71
  planning, 25
  See also training
educational institutions, 53, 58
  cluster surveys, 81–82, 84
  Indonesia, 162
  reproductive health, 120–21
  supervision, 146
efficiency, 164
  hospitals, 151–52
  Kenya, 146–47
  private sector, 166
  See also cost-effectiveness
employment. *See* human resources
empowerment, 21, 127
epidemiologists, 53, 161
epidemiology, 20, 66
equipment, 28–29, 144
  hospitals, 140
  quality of care, 97
  reproductive health, 118
  See also supplies
equity of access, 12, 34
essential drug lists (EDL), 66, 70, 121

European Commission human resources analysis, 61

facilities, 28–29, 97, 144
family planning, 5, 118, 184
  Africa, 124
  cluster surveys, 81
  Colombia, 117
  contraceptive prevalence surveys, 83
  data collection, 81, 83, 92
  Indonesia, 158–59
  integration of services, 127–29
  management information systems, 73–92
  monitoring, 77*fig*, 91
  Philippines, 74–76, 79–80, 84–85, 86–87*table*, 91, 93–94n9, 117
  Social Marketing of Contraceptives Project, 76
  surveys, 79–89
  sustainability, 77, 121
Family Planning Management Development project, 91, 93–94n9
fees, 32–34, 149
female genital mutilation, 113
feminist organizations, 116–18
FHSIS. *See* Field Health Services Information System
Field Health Services Information System (FHSIS), 5, 73–74
  comparison of methods, 80
  local levels, 80, 91–92
  modifications, 76
  provincial levels, 81
  reliability, 76
financial aspects, 3–4, 17, 27–36, 58
  Cause and Effect in Decentralization, 28*fig*
  cost-sharing, 142–43
  Departments of Health, 105–6
  devolution, 28–31
  hospitals, 137, 140, 151–52
  human resources, 57–61
  Indonesia, 160
  Kenya, 146*table*
  Kenyatta National Hospital, 148–49

Papua New Guinea, 141–42
  pharmaceutical management, 68–70, 100
  Philippines, 30–31, 31*fig*, 36
  planning, 14
  regional/provincial levels, 124–25
  reproductive health, 118–19, 123
  training, 98–99
  travel allowances, 57, 99, 104, 106, 141–42
  See also cost-effectiveness; donors
Fiscal Impact of Devolution in the Philippines, 31*fig*
Fully Immunized Children 12 to 59 Months of Age, 88–89*table*

Gadjah Mada University (Indonesia), 157
Gambia, 139, 142
Ghana, 124, 140–41
Gilson, Lucy, 50–51
goals. *See* planning
governance, 17
Guinea, 183

Haiti, 183
Harvard School of Public Health, 2
health care workers, 14, 17, 54, 97, 99
  career development, 52–53
  empowerment, 20
  family planning, 130
  hospitals, 137
  human resources, 50–53
  integration of services, 128–29
  morale and motivation, 42, 47–48
  job security, 46, 50, 103, 106, 120, 130, 146
  lawbreakers, 16, 24
  reproductive health, 117–18
  See also human resources; staffing; training
health centers. *See* local levels
health economists, 53
health facility assessments, 90–91
health insurance, 3–4, 30, 123, 151–52

health management information systems, 73–92
  See also management information systems
Health Project IV (HP-IV), 8, 157–158, 168
health reform, 183
health systems, 121–26
  See also organizational structures
hiring. *See* staffing
HIV. *See* human immune deficiency virus (HIV)
horizontal integration, 128
hospitals, 7–8, 137–52
  autonomous, 36, 144–52
  boards of directors, 50, 140–41
  data collection, 141
  efficiency, 146–48
  equipment, 140, 144
  facilities, 144
  financial aspects, 139–43
  Gambia, 142
  human resources, 137, 140, 143
  integration of services, 139–40
  Kenya, 35, 142–43, 146–48
  management, 139–41
  managers, 50, 141
  pharmaceutical management, 65, 143–44
  planning, 140
  primary health services, 141–42
  staffing, 49, 143, 151–52
  standards of care, 140
  supervision, 140
  supplies, 140, 143–44
  teaching, 139
  utilization, 122
  vertical integration, 122–23
  See also Kenyatta National Hospital
HP-IV. *See* Health Project IV
human immune deficiency virus (HIV), 113, 118
  Africa, 124
  incidence, 114
  integration of services, 126–27
human relations, 118
human resources, 4, 39–61
  career development, 52–53, 58

conflict-resolution mechanisms, 48
data collection, 51, 58–61
decision making, 59–60
devolution, 41
hiring, 45
hospitals, 137, 140, 143, 151–52
Indonesia, 160, 168
job descriptions, 43–44
job security, 120, 146
Kenya, 33, 35 146*table*
Kenyatta National Hospital, 146
legal aspects, 58
management, 53–55, 57–61
monitoring, 61
morale and motivation, 42, 47–48, 97, 99–100, 103, 106
organizational structures, 41, 43–44, 48–50, 58
Pan American Health Organization matrix, 61
pensions, 146
performance assessments, 58, 60
performance conditions, 55–57, 60, 129
personnel management, 43–45, 58–59
Philippines, 28–30
planning, 58
reallocation of staff, 41–43, 45, 51, 54
reproductive health, 120–21
salaries and benefits, 44, 58, 120
staffing, 14, 42–46, 53–54, 58, 102–3, 120
supervision, 50, 54–55, 57, 97–99
technical skills, 53–55
training, 52–54, 58, 60, 120–21
transfers, 42–46, 52, 58, 103, 120
Workload Indicators of Need, 60
World Health Organization toolkit, 61, 64n27
See also health care workers
Human Resources for Health Development Journal, 4
human rights, 6–7

ICPD. *See* International Conference on Population and Development
immunization
 Indonesia, 158–59, 165
 integration of services, 128
 Philippines, 6, 85, 88–89*table*, 104–5, 107–8n2
 surveys, 83
 tetanus, 161–62
implementation, 17, 21, 95
India, 127, 166
Indonesia, 8, 157–69
 block grants, 166, 168
 central/national levels, 166–68
 Comprehensive Health Improvement Project— Province Specific (CHIPPS), 161–63
 computerization, 165
 data collection, 159, 161–62, 168
 district levels, 159, 166–67
 donors, 168
 drugs, 100, 162
 educational institutions, 162
 family planning, 158–59
 financial aspects, 160, 167–68
 human resources, 160–66
 immunization, 158–59, 165
 integration of services, 164
 local levels, 162, 166–67
 management information systems, 159
 planning, 160, 168
 primary health care, 96
 private sector, 164, 166
 program development, 159
 provincial levels, 159
 quality assurance, 164
 quality of care, 95–96
 staffing, 168
 supervision, 160, 162
 sustainability, 162–63
 training, 161–62, 165–66
 US Agency for International Development, 168
 World Bank, 168
inequity, 12, 34
infant mortality, 114
infertility, 114
innovation, 14, 22–23
See also planning

Integrated Management of Childhood Illness (course), 98
integration of services
 central/national levels, 129–31
 horizontal, 128
 hospitals, 139–40
 Indonesia, 164
 Philippines, 138
 referral networks, 34, 97–98, 101, 114
 reproductive health, 122–31
 training, 128–29
 vertical, 122–23
international agreements, 66, 75
international assistance. *See* donors
International Conference on Harmonization, 66
International Conference on Population and Development (ICPD), 2, 7, 111, 131
International Dispensary Association (IDA), 67

job security, 46, 50, 103, 106
 family planning, 130
 Kenyatta National Hospital, 146
 reproductive health, 120

Kenya, 3–4, 27, 31–36, 183
 administrative aspects, 33–35
 budgeting, 33
 cost-sharing, 27–28, 31–36, 32*fig*, 142–43
 district levels, 27–28, 33
 drug procurement, 33
 economic aspects, 31–32
 equity of access, 34
 family planning, 129–30
 fees, 32–34
 hospital autonomy, 36, 144–52
 hospitals, 7–8, 35, 142–43
 human resources, 33
 policy formulation, 35
 political aspects, 31–32
 primary health care, 33
 public education, 32–33
 referral patterns, 34

Index 179

staffing, 35
training, 34
Kenyatta National Hospital, 36, 144–52
  Distribution of Authority Before and After KNH Became a State Corporation, 146*table*
KNH. *See* Kenyatta National Hospital
Kolehmainen-Aitken, Riitta-Liisa, 4, 14, 61n1; 62nn4, 6, 12; 63nn13, 14, 17; 63–64n25; 64n26; 133n17; 134nn26; 29, 30; 153, 171, 174

Labor Force Surveys, 92
labor relations, 42, 44–47
  Philippines, 56–57, 103–4
Laing, Richard, 4–5, 172–73
leadership, 22–23
legal aspects, 3, 24, 58
legislation, 16
LGU. *See* local levels
LGU Performance Program, 92
local levels
  cluster surveys, 83–84
  control, 18–19, 54
  data collection, 74, 163
  drug procurement, 67, 100
  family planning, 80, 130
  Family Planning Management Development project, 91, 93–94n9
  fees, 69
  financial aspects, 141–42
  Health Project IV, 163–67
  hospitals, 140, 142–43, 151
  Indonesia, 158, 162, 166–67
  information needs, 80–81
  management information systems, 125, 163
  managers, 50
  maternal and child health, 80
  monitoring, 73, 91–92
  pharmaceutical management, 69–70
  Philippines, 75
  planners, 21
  planning, 13–14
  roles, 59, 105–6
  staff skills, 52, 54
  staffing, 58

supervision, 104–5
training, 54, 125
utilization of services, 80–81
vertical integration, 122–23
long-range goals, 20
See also planning

Macro International, 79
Madagascar, 184
Magboo, Florante, 5, 173
Malaysia, 123
management, 3, 16–17
  hospitals, 139, 151–52
  human resources, 4, 53–55, 57–61
  integrated services, 126–31
  Kenya, 146*table*
  Kenyatta National Hospital, 145–47
  minimum management package, 79
  political aspects, 124
  reproductive health, 123–25
  training, 123–24, 150, 183
  See also managers
management information systems, 73–92, 125, 183
  hospitals, 140–41
  Indonesia, 159
  Kenyatta National Hospital, 146
  reproductive health, 125
  staffing issues, 146
  sustainability, 92
  See also data collection; surveys
Management Sciences for Health, 2, 28, 40, 183–84
  monitoring strategies, 76–78, 77*fig*
managers, 23
  doctors, 50
  hospitals, 140, 150–51
  human resources, 55, 57–61
  qualifications, 140, 165
  quality of care, 96–97
  skills, 53–55
  See also management
Marcos, Ferdinand, 29, 102
maternal and child health (MCH), 5, 183
  Africa, 124
  cluster surveys, 81
  management information systems, 73–92

monitoring strategies, 77*fig*
  prenatal care, 128–29
  surveys, 79–81
  See also family planning; reproductive health
Maternal and Child Health Technical Assistance (TASC), 184
maternal care, 118
maternal mortality, 112–14
medical technology, 39
Mexico, 45, 117, 127
MICS. *See* multi-indicator cluster surveys
minimum management package, 79
Ministries of Health, 13, 40, 42
  Philippines, 44, 78–79, 83, 105–6
mixed decentralization, 151
monitoring strategies, 5
  data collection, 77–78
  Family Planning Management Development project, 94–95n9
  local levels, 73, 91–92
  See also data collection; management information systems
morale and motivation, 97, 103, 106
  human resources, 42, 47–48
  quality of care, 99–100
multi-indicator cluster surveys, 82–84
  See also cluster surveys

National Health and Demographic Surveys, 79–80
national level. *See* central/national levels
Nepal, 44, 130
Newbrander, William, 7–8, 14, 37n7; 61n1; 62nn6; 12; 63n14, 63–64n25; 133n17; 134nn25, 29, 30; 152n1; 153, 173-74
Nicaragua, 52, 115
  hospitals, 50, 123, 138
Nigeria, 115, 119
nongovernmental organizations, 119, 130
Northrup, Robert, 8, 169n2, 174

nurses, 55
nutrition services, 7*fig*, 113

organizational structures, 40, 121–26
  horizontal integration, 128
  human resources, 43–44
  integrated services, 126–31
  pharmaceutical management, 66
  roles and responsibilities, 48–50
  vertical integration, 30, 122–23, 158–59, 167

Pan American Health Organization human resources matrix, 61
Papua New Guinea, 42–43, 48, 51
  civil service, 44, 52
  data collection, 51
  facilities and equipment, 144
  family planning, 131
  financial aspects, 141–42
  hospitals, 139
  organizational structures, 49
  performance conditions, 56–57
  reproductive health, 119, 121, 124
  staffing, 45, 51
  supervision, 55, 122–23
  training, 54
  vertical integration, 122
Partnership for Child Health Care, Inc., 184
patronage, 103, 151–52
pensions, 146
performance assessments, 60
performance conditions, 55–57, 60, 99–100
  hospitals, 143
  integration of services, 129
personnel. *See* human resources
pharmaceutical management, 4–5, 65–71, 183
  central/national levels, 69–70
  distribution, 68, 70
  financial aspects, 68–70, 100
  hospitals, 143–44
  human resources, 39, 70

procurement, 67, 70
quality assurance, 69–70
quality of care, 97, 100
regulations, 69
reproductive health, 121
Selection Issues, 67*fig*
PHC. *See* primary health care
Philippines, 3–6, 27–31, 29*fig*, 31*fig*, 96, 115, 157, 183
  central/national level, 75
  certification, 90–91
  contraceptive use, 74, 79–80, 83
  Demographic and Health Surveys, 77
  Department of Health, 44, 78–79, 83, 105–6
  devolution, 27–31, 73, 75*table*
  donors, 85
  drug procurement, 30–31, 143–44
  Expanded Programme on Immunization, 83
  facilities and equipment, 28–29
  family planning, 74–76, 79–80, 84–85, 86–87*table*, 91, 93–94n9, 117
  fertility rate, 74–75
  financial aspects, 30–31, 36
  health facility assessments, 90–91
  health insurance, 30
  hospitals, 138
  human resources, 28–30, 46, 56–57, 78, 101–5
  immunization, 6, 85, 88–89 *table*, 104–5, 107–8n2
  integration of services, 138
  labor demonstrations, 103–4
  Labor Force Surveys, 79–80
  local level services, 73, 75
  maternal and child health, 75, 79–80
  mortality rates, 74
  national campaigns, 15
  National Health and Demographic Surveys, 79–80
  organizational structures, 30, 49, 123
  planning, 36
  policies and procedures, 31
  political aspects, 29
  primary health care, 75

provincial level services, 75
quality of care, 101–6
reproductive health, 117, 120–21, 124
salaries and benefits, 30, 78
staffing, 28–29, 46, 101–2
supervision, 104–5
supplies, 28–29, 143–44
surveys, 78–80
training, 98
transfers, 46
physicians. *See* doctors
pilot tests, 75
planners, 12–13, 18–21, 24, 161
  central vs. decentralized, 18–21
  roles, 18–19, 24
planning, 3, 11–25, 150
  annual comprehensive plans, 90–91
  capacity building, 35
  financial aspects, 124
  goals and objectives, 16
  guidelines, 22–25
  hospitals, 140
  human resources, 53, 58
  Indonesia, 157–58, 160, 168
  local levels, 80–81
  Philippines, 36
  priorities, 24–25, 40
  quality of care, 106
  reproductive health, 124
  staffing, 58
  See also management information systems
policies, 6–7, 12–13, 15
  Kenya, 35, 78, 146*table*
  Philippines, 31
  reform, 39–40
  reproductive health, 116–18
political aspects, 3, 12, 20–21, 24, 40–41
  abortion, 117
  certification, 90
  family planning, 130–31
  hospital autonomy, 150–51
  hospitals, 140
  human resources, 43–44, 51
  Indonesia, 168–69
  Kenya, 31–32
  organizational structures, 43–44
  patronage, 103, 151–52
  Philippines, 29, 102

quality of care, 103
reproductive health, 111, 116–18, 120
staffing, 102–3
supervision, 55, 104–5
polypharmacy, 69, 162
population mobility, 124
populations at risk, 81
Potential Benefits and Drawbacks of Decentralization, 14*table*
power. *See* control
Pratt, Robert, 158
prenatal care. *See* maternal and child health
preventive health care, 39
primary health care, 73–74, 183
hospitals, 141–42
Kenya, 33
Kenyatta National Hospital, 149
pharmaceutical management, 65
private sector, 164, 166
privatization, 65*def*
procurement, 146*table*
See also drugs; equipment; supplies
professional associations, 42, 46–47
program development, 21, 159
projects, five-year, 169
provincial/regional levels
cluster surveys, 81–84
Comprehensive Health Improvement Project—Province Specific (CHIPPS), 157, 161–63
data collection, 74
family planning, 130
financial aspects, 124–25, 139
hospitals, 104, 139
Indonesia, 157, 159, 161–63
organizational structures, 49, 123
Philippines, 75
supervision, 104
training, 121, 124–25
public education. *See* education
public relations, 149

quality assurance, 5, 36, 70, 121, 140, 164
quality of care, 5–6, 14, 95–107, 164
certification, 107
data collection, 81
Department of Health (Philippines), 105–6
hospitals, 151–52
Kenyatta National Hospital, 149
morale and motivation, 99–100
point of service, 96–97
private sector, 166
referral networks, 97–98
supervision, 99
training, 98–99

recentralization, 139
referral networks, 97–98, 101
Kenya, 34
maternal mortality, 114
vertical integration, 122–23
reform, 39–40
regional levels. *See* provincial/regional levels
registration bodies, 42, 46–47
regulations, 75
pharmaceuticals, 5, 67, 69–71
Reilly, Quentin, 42–43
reimbursement, 123
rent-seeking behavior, 13, 25n2
reproductive health, 2, 6–7, 111–32, 112*def*, 183
abortion, 112–13
accessibility, 117–18
acquired immune deficiency syndrome, 113
financial aspects, 118–19
goals, 118
human immune deficiency virus, 113
implementation, 118–31
maternal mortality, 112–14
Philippines, 120–21
political aspects, 111
quality of care, 118
sexually transmitted diseases, 113
See also family planning; maternal and child health
resource allocation, 14, 90–91
Kenya, 147–49

Rodriguez, Jose, 5, 174–75
roles and responsibilities. *See* central/national levels; local levels; provincial/regional levels
Rondinelli, Dennis, 65

safety, 126–27
salaries and benefits, 44, 58, 103, 106
hospitals, 143
Kenya, 146*table*
Kenyatta National Hospital, 146, 148
Philippines, 30
reproductive health, 120
sampling methods, 82–83
self-instructional materials, 99
Senegal, 184
service delivery, 90–92, 96–97
fragmentation, 12
See also integration of services
service standards. *See* quality assurance
sex education, 113
sexually transmitted diseases (STDs), 113–14, 118, 124
integration of services, 126–29
See also human immune deficiency virus
Social Marketing of Contraceptives Project, 76
Solter, Steven, 5–6, 158, 175
South Africa, 50, 183
Sri Lanka, 46
staff. *See* health care workers; human resources
staff development. *See* training
staffing, 14, 42–46, 53–54, 58, 102–3, 120
hospitals, 49, 143, 151–52
Indonesia, 168
Kenya, 35, 146*table*
Kenyatta National Hospital, 146
Philippines, 28–29
turnover, 54
Workload Indicators of Need, 60
standards of care, 36, 140
standard treatment guidelines, 70
statistical sampling methods, 82–83

Stover, Charles, 3–4, 175–76
strategic planning. *See* planning processes
supervision, 54–55, 141–42
  doctors, 50, 55, 146
  hospitals, 140, 143
  Indonesia, 160, 162
  pharmaceutical management, 70
  Philippines, 104
  planning, 14
  quality of care, 97, 101
  travel allowances, 57, 99, 104, 106, 141–42
supplies
  hospitals, 140, 143–44, 151–52
  Kenyatta National Hospital, 147–48
  Philippines, 28–29
  quality of care, 97
  reproductive health, 121
surveys. *See* data collection
sustainability, 77, 92, 121, 162–63
synergy, 127

Tanzania, 51
teaching hospitals, 139
technical skills, 53–55
  cluster surveys, 83
  Kenyatta National Hospital, 149–50
  management, 123–24
  reproductive health, 118
  See also training
tetanus, 161–62
Timmons, Robert, 5, 176
training, 17, 52–53, 58, 60
  boards of directors, 140–41
  funding, 98–99
  health facility assessments, 90–91
  hospitals, 140, 143
  human resources, 39
  Indonesia, 161–62, 165–66
  integration of services, 128–29
  Kenya, 34
  pharmaceutical management, 66, 70
  planning, 19, 25
  problem solving, 166
  quality of care, 97–99
  reproductive health, 120–21, 124
transfers, 42–46, 58, 103, 120
transportation systems, 122–23
travel allowances, 57, 99, 104, 141–42
tuberculosis, 124, 162
Tunisia, 127

United Nations Children's Fund (UNICEF), 83
unions, 42, 46–47
  see also labor relations
urban concerns, 124–25
US Agency for International Development (USAID), 8
  Basic Support for Institutionalizing Child Survival (BASICS), 184
  Center for Population, Health, and Nutrition, 77–78
  commodities distribution and logistics MIS, 80
  Comprehensive Health Improvement Project—Province Specific, 157, 161–63
  data collection, 83–84, 92
  Indonesia, 158, 168
  Kenyatta National Hospital, 148, 150
  Macro International, 79
  Management Sciences for Health, 28 183
  monitoring primary health care, 74
  National Health and Demograhic Surveys, 79–80
USAID. *See* US Agency for International Development

utilization of services, 69, 80–81, 91–92, 164

vertical integration, 30, 158–59, 167
  local levels, 122–23
vitamin A distribution, 104–5, 108n3
volunteers, 125–26

WHO. *See* World Health Organization
working conditions. *See* performance conditions
Workload Indicators of Staffing Need, 60
World Bank, 8, 39, 112
  Community Health and Nutrition III (CHN-III), 157
  Health Project IV, 157, 163–67
  Indonesia, 157, 168
  Kenyatta National Hospital, 150
  World Development Report, 112
World Health Organization (WHO), 2
  human resources, 50
  human resources toolkit, 61, 64n27
  reproductive health, 112*def*
World Trade Organization
  pharmaceutical management, 66

Zambia, 157, 168
  civil service, 46
  hospitals, 122
  organizational structures, 123
  reproductive health, 120, 124
  training, 53

About Management Sciences for Health

Management Sciences for Health, Inc. (MSH), is a private, nonprofit organization, dedicated to closing the gap between what is known about public health problems and what is done to solve them. Since 1971, MSH has collaborated with health decision-makers throughout the world to improve the quality, availability, and affordability of health and population services.

MSH has assisted public and private health and population programs in over 100 countries by providing technical assistance, conducting training, carrying out applied research, and developing systems for health program management. MSH maintains a staff of over 300 in its Boston, Massachusetts headquarters, offices in Washington, DC, and field offices throughout the world.

We provide long- and short-term technical assistance in six areas of expertise:

- primary health care and maternal/child health
- population and reproductive health
- health reform and financing
- information for management
- management training
- drug management

Recent and ongoing major efforts by MSH to address problems in public health include the following:

- MSH currently manages two multinational projects funded by the US Agency for International Development (Family Planning Management Development and Rational Pharmaceutical Management).
- MSH is also carrying out several national projects, including three in Africa (Guinea, Kenya, and South Africa), one in Haiti, and one in the Philippines.

- We recently concluded successful work on the Madagascar APPROPOP/Family Planning and Senegal Child Survival and Family Planning projects.
- MSH is one of three members of the Partnership for Child Health Care, Inc., which implements USAID's flagship child survival project, Basic Support for Institutionalizing Child Survival (BASICS).
- We have also been awarded a contract to carry out global technical assistance under the Maternal Child Health Technical Assistance (TASC) activity.